The
HEART
of
LISTENING

The
HEART
of
LISTENING

CRIS SMITH

Copyright © 2013 by Cris Smith.

Library of Congress Control Number: 2013901288
ISBN: Hardcover   978-1-4797-8289-5
              Softcover   978-1-4797-8175-1
              Ebook   978-1-4797-8176-8

All rights reserved. No part of this book may be reproduced or transmitted in any form or by any means, electronic or mechanical, including photocopying, recording, or by any information storage and retrieval system, without permission in writing from the copyright owner.

Cover Design by Paolo Rinaldi
Cover Photos by Anil Sankat

This book was printed in the United States of America.

Rev. date: 03/28/2013

To order additional copies of this book, contact:
Xlibris Corporation
1-888-795-4274
www.Xlibris.com
Orders@Xlibris.com
119307

Contents

Acknowledgment 9
Author's Message: Can You Hear Me?.................................11
Foreword..13

Chapter 1:   Reflection in the Mirror . . . ."I AM"................15
Chapter 2:   "Be Still and Know" 19
Chapter 3:   "Perfect Love Casts out Fear" 1 John 4:18 22
Chapter 4:   Guide My Way...25
Chapter 5:   Human Angels in Our Midst 29
Chapter 6:   Nightly Dramas..32
Chapter 7:   Love Language 37
Chapter 8:   Soul Imprints 42
Chapter 9:   The Impact of Giving..44
Chapter 10: Out of the Mouth of a Child............................46
Chapter 11: A Spirit Filled Moment 50
Chapter 12: Treasured Gifts 53
Chapter 13: Supernatural...57
Chapter 14: Miracle 62
Chapter 15: Held in the Palm of His Hand 67
Chapter 16: Reliving Happy Moments 72
Chapter 17: Stirring in my Heart..76
Chapter 18: Secret Code of Love...86

Journal Writing 91
Dream Journal...93
Something About The Author 95
My Family..99
Journal Reflections 103

This book is in tribute to
Sara Elizabeth Smith
April 15, 1997 - May 11, 1997

"**The Heart of Listening**", inspired from the author's original manuscript entitled, "Let the Spirit Fly Wherever it Takes You" . . . Fr. Occhio's comment . . . . "one of the very finest inspirational books I have ever read in my entire life. No, Cris did not have St. Augustine's "wild" youth but her writing style and approach is somewhat reminiscent of the great Saint's Confessions. Children, married couples, parents, teachers, catechists, and any perceptive reader looking for down-to-earth ways of handing down perennial values to the new generations will find in these pages educational and spiritual insights of the highest caliber." Fr. Joseph M. Occhio, SDB, STL, Ph.D

"I truly believe a modern day prophet has appeared in our midst." Maureen Timms

"The whole time I was reading I kept thinking that this book could be such an inspiration to so many, and have phenomenal impact on someone doubtful or searching for God. I find that the chapters have a message of their own and can definitely be read independently. I think the detail expresses the author's feelings, emotions, love and how her faith has sustained and led her . . . a book . . . truly God inspired." Alisia Sabatini

"The Heart of Listening", allowed me to think back and reflect on my own past experiences where God has revealed himself to me in my life. Each chapter was informative and captured my attention through the brief, yet powerful encounters you had experienced with family, friends, strangers, the dying and the supernatural. Your own personal journey opens the doors for others to get to know you the writer, Cris Smith, on a deeper and more personal level, and yet forces them to look at their own life experiences and reinforces that they too are not alone in this walk of life. Thanks for sharing your book with me!" Santina DiMatteo

"There are a few authors, if any, like Cris. "The Heart of Listening" had a profound effect on my thoughts, heart and soul—it even motivated me to keep my own journal! By truly opening up in these journal entries and sharing such intimate details of her life, Cris not only made me reflect upon my own life, but forced me to explore the fundamentals. Her stories continue to inspire me to "listen" daily—I can honestly say this is an unforgettable and remarkable book."—Rona Chavez

Acknowledgment

With a spirit of gratitude I acknowledge my sister Mary Rinaldi who is responsible for the original fine-tuning of this book. Without her invaluable help I know that I would not be able to complete many of the projects I am inspired to begin. She is always there for me to listen with her heart and without judgment. She has been there to support me and my family—in particular my 9 children—with unconditional love. Her encouragement, along with her energy and passion in finding opportunities to help people discover and live their life dreams, is truly her gift. I am forever grateful for her involvement in my life and her contribution of making the vision of the Sara Elizabeth Centre a reality.

This book could not have been completed without the contribution of Paolo Rinaldi's beautiful artwork, illustration and cover design. His masterful perception of my words was expressed beyond my imagining. I thank him for sharing his great smile, praise him for his humble spirit and pray for his continued success in all that God entrusts into his hands.

I am so grateful to Rona Chavez for her invaluable contribution in producing the final edit. Her praise for my writing blessed and inspired me. I thank her for her contagious spirit of joy and positive disposition. Her support, amazing flexibility and encouragement are something I looked forward to, along with her helpful comments, input, corrections and finally her stamp of approval. I am blessed to have Rona in my life and pray she will continue to walk with me as we serve the Lord.

I thank all my spiritual friends on earth and in heaven who share their light with me. They include the Salesians, prayer warriors, soul sisters, co-workers and even strangers who God has sent into my life as messengers of love, guidance, direction, moral support, acceptance and encouragement.

I owe my life story to my family, in particular my children Jeff, Phill, Donny, David, Joseph, Jonathan, Mary-Ann, Sara, and Stephanie. I include my daughters-in-law, Santina and Amber and all future members of my family who have not yet joined us. I cannot forget my grandchildren, Christian, Sabastian and Matteo and my dad, Antonio Orsini. Honourable mention also goes to my siblings, Lucy, Mary, and Frank, their spouses Domenic and Angie, my nieces and nephews and all my extended family too numerous to mention who have shared in my life experiences. They are truly God's instruments in helping me testify to HIS love. And last, but certainly never least, I must thank Don my husband, my soul mate, who shares my secret code of love, and my best friend!

A special thank you to the Sara Elizabeth Centre's board of directors, supporters and families who have blessed us with their moral and financial support, their participation and presence, gifts and talents, and ultimately their unity in living our motto, "Where everyone can shine like a star! A special thank you goes to Cathy Turco, member of the board of directors, parent and soul sister, who upon her return from a pilgrimage to the Holy Land brought back a special gift for me that confirmed how much God loves us all!

Finally I thank my God who created me with a purpose and gave me a future full of hope, ensuring that I would not walk this path alone! I am truly blessed!

Author's Message:

Can You Hear Me?

On a cold winter's morning in January 2006, my sons, Jeff, Phil, Donny and David are rehearsing songs they have just recently composed. In a few weeks, they will head out to the studio to record these songs, to create an album with proceeds going to the Sara Elizabeth Centre, a youth centre helping young adults with developmental and physical disabilities, run by a nonprofit charity called Blue Veil.

As I work in the kitchen, I hear my sons jamming downstairs. Jeff is strumming a new tune on his guitar and singing lyrics I have never heard before. The piano keys join in as David adds a note, Donny contributes with a lead chord and another verse while Phil keeps the tempo with his drums and jymbe. After a few hours, I hear the harmonies coming together to complete a song as each brother brings new meaning to this melodic creation.

Weeks later, they are in the studio as planned. They begin the process of recording the ten songs they have finished composing. All the songs resonate a recurring theme of love, faith, hope and unity. By the end of the first day, they manage to get through two soundtracks. The next few days continue to unfold, the energy is high and they manage to finish recording the remaining songs for the album entitled "Leap of Faith". It is now the last day scheduled in the recording studio and Donny asks his brothers to listen to 'one more' song he has just finished writing. He hopes it fits with this project. He begins to strum the chords softly on his classical guitar and sings the lyrics of what becomes their last song on the album. The song is entitled "Guide My Way" and becomes track 11 on the album. The chorus in this song repeats a heartfelt question—"Can you hear me?" This question is one that so many of us have asked at one time or another. In my personal experience, I know I have, as I searched for a sense of purpose and direction in my early teens. I searched for answers to questions regarding my identity, my reason for being, and even my faith. I questioned if someone could really hear me when I prayed, when I had strange thoughts, or when I wished for things to happen or appear. As a grownup I began to ask less and less, until that memorable day almost fifteen years ago when I gave birth to a dying child. Heartbroken, I began to ask questions again, looking for answers that lay deep within my soul. Thankfully, through my pain and sorrow I came to recognize that still small voice that spoke directly to my heart. I listened and discovered meaning through signs, symbols, dreams, visions, prayers and direct manifestations. Simply by opening the ears of my heart, I discovered how to really listen. Today, I know that I no longer walk alone as I continue on my journey. In union with that still, small voice, I can experience peace and joy while still remaining focused and positive.

The album "Leap of Faith" is completed and "Guide My Way, Track No. 11, becomes the nucleus that helps and encourages me to take quite a significant leap of faith and write "The Heart of Listening". Each chapter is intended to get you thinking of your own personal experiences. In a spirit of anticipating joy, may you discover that you have been guided to this very moment in which you will hopefully come to hear what you have been waiting for and continue to grow in the art of listening simply by listening with the ears of your heart.

Foreword

The first time I heard a voice I ignored it. The second time I wondered who it was. The third time I decided to listen! Cris Smith

I have mastered the art of multitasking simply because of my role as a mother of 9 children and my involvement with youth as a retreat facilitator. However, my ability to listen was not at the same level until the birth of my 8th child. During this time, it felt like a veil had been lifted and I discovered how much my heart needed healing not only from the pain of losing her shortly after her birth, but from the emotions of fear and guilt that surface in times like these. I began to embark on a journey which included me searching for answers. Why?" Why did I have to experience this loss? Why did I have to experience such heartfelt emotions that could not be described in words? Taking time to heal, I found the need to stop, rest, pray, and connect with my loved ones. In return, I discovered a new connection with something that lifted me up and carried me through. In the midst of my sorrow, I was experiencing joy as I began to hear what I longed for.

This was 15 years ago. Today, I continue to find time to stop frequently from my hectic schedule and just listen. No matter what stage of life you are in now, I wish to share with you in the next few chapters some of my stories that helped me in my discovery of listening with the ear of my heart. You will find that we are all connected to each other by a powerful Source. This Source will reveal itself to you when you are prepared to truly listen. Listening is a dialogue and not a monologue—so take the time to stop, listen, meditate and reflect. Pause often as you read and think about what is being mentioned as it applies to you and your life. You will discover that the secret to listening is to listen with the ear of your h **e a r** t.

Chapter 1

Reflection in the Mirror...."I AM"

As a small child back in Italy I was baptized into the Catholic faith. Months later my parents immigrated to Canada and for years found themselves moving from one place to another until they were able to settle into a permanent dwelling they could call their own. Attending church or remaining connected to a community—outside of our family and relatives—was difficult, but we stuck together, living together and helping each other survive in this new country. By the time I was six, I was ready for my First Holy Communion and aside from attending a few sacramental blessings, such as the baptisms of my siblings, or festive occasions like, Christmas and Easter, our family hardly went to church. In fact, these occasions and attending Catholic school was what I believed meant to be a Catholic.

Not having had a personal relationship with God growing up, left me searching for answers. It wasn't until years later, when things were at their worst in my life and I had reached a point of desperation I understood the meaning behind the gifts of the Holy Spirit. The responsibilities of being married and raising a family together with my husband began to take a toll on our love for each other. My strength was gone, my hope lost and my ability to carry on was on the brinks. We both knew something was missing, but with two kids, a mortgage, a job and a husband who worked two jobs to keep us going, we discovered that we had little time to do anything else, let alone find the time for God or know how to fit Him into our hectic schedules.

THE REFLECTION IN THE MIRROR: I will never forget what happened to me at work one morning as I stood in front of the mirror in the women's washroom. This experience was a real climatic turning point in my life—a realization of God was present. It seemed as though time stood still, as I stood staring at my reflection. In that brief moment, I saw myself detach from my body. It was as if I was floating in the form of a spirit. Then, deep within me, I heard the words, "I AM". I snapped back to reality with a new awareness that 'I AM' God's child. I am not just a body but I am a spirit too, united with the great 'I AM. At the time this occurred, I was in my thirties, but in spirit I felt I was still a very young child. Little did I know I was beginning my walk with God that day, a walk that would later lead me towards my first step in having a personal relationship with Jesus.

In the days and months that followed this experience, I began to feel an inexplicable urgency to return back to my church. I recall how my husband, Don and I visited other worship dwellings through business associates of ours, who were Born Again Christians. As I look back to one service in particular, I recall how Don and I accepted the altar call to give ourselves to Jesus and how we allowed the preacher to pray for our salvation as he invited Jesus into our lives. I believe Jesus knew that my husband and I really didn't understand what we were doing back then, and even though we never returned to any more of those worship services, Don and I still felt we both needed to continue searching. I believe the Lord knew this and gently took us by the hand helping us embark on this new journey that would allow us to find Him.

My husband and I first realized Jesus was leading us to Him, when we received an invitation in my church's bulletin to participate in a Marriage Encounter weekend, where married couples learned how to deepen their relationship with one another and with God. At this point in our lives both of us were burned out from all the self-imposed expectations of our daily lives. Our day consisted of, waking up very early in the morning, dressing the kids, dragging them half asleep to the car, driving an hour to drop them off at my mom's house (who babysat for us), then driving another 30 minutes to get to work. Needless to say, even before I started work I was ready for my morning break! Then after working eight long hours, the evening ritual began with the same hectic pace as my morning. Only this time with a few additional chores added to the list. With all of this on my plate, there was hardly ever any time for myself, my kids or my husband, let alone God.

We continued this bizarre daily ritual of travelling back and forth with our kids, until I became pregnant with our third child and my energy levels dropped during my fourth month. Many evenings my family never even made it home. Instead, we just took up residence at my parents' home, imposing on them and taking advantage of their generosity, even though they never said so.

So, needless to say, when the opportunity came for a weekend away, my husband and I agreed it would be a great opportunity for us to catch up on some much needed sleep. Little did we know how busy we would be on this blessed weekend where silence was the rule between other couples but much communication was expected between husband and wife. Our facilitators consisted of a priest and two other couples that helped us discover ourselves, our relationship with each other and our relationship with God. I discovered that by loving my husband, I was also loving God and myself and that through the vocation of marriage I was fulfilling my role as a mother, wife and, above all, God's child.

After the 'Marriage Encounter' weekend, our daily routine did not change dramatically, but what did change was the way Don and I now communicated with each other, listening and understanding each other better and we realized how important is was to include Sunday worship in our lives. This experience opened our hearts to see God in our lives each day and to see that we belonged to a community of family, friends and neighbours, that all came together at church. That year, many wonderful blessings were bestowed on my family. Not only had we discovered we were now part of a community in Christ, but shortly after this, my husband announced he wanted to convert into the Catholic faith.

Since my husband's conversion and our 'Marriage Encounter' weekend, I have never looked back or doubted my decision to follow that still small voice inside my heart. I know now it was God, the 'I AM', I was searching for and that He never intended for me to be separated from Him. I can joyfully say, "I sought the Lord, and He heard me, and delivered me from all my fears." Psalm 34:4

Perhaps you too have immigrated to this country or you know someone like your parents or grandparents who immigrated years ago. Imagine how they must have felt as they landed in this new land either as newlyweds or with young children and not speaking a word of English. As frightening as this may have been for them, they somehow learned how to survive all the challenges that came with being separated from their family and friends. Settling in this new land, promised them a new life of freedom and employment but it also meant they would have to adapt to a new culture and learn a new language . . . yet they courageously moved forward. How? They listened to their hearts and took a leap of faith embarking on this new journey where they formed a new community of family and friends.

Chapter 2

"Be Still and Know"

I give you the desires of your heart, says the Lord. The more we want to hear God and listen, the more we will hear.

In a dream I had one evening, I heard a voice gently telling me to, **"Remain still."** Upon awakening the next morning, I discerned that the voice was that of the Lord's speaking to me and giving me a profound message in one simple statement. Then in another dream on the following evening, I saw myself standing in the center of a main road. Suddenly, the earth beneath my feet began to tremble and shake and as I looked out into the road I saw the pavement cracking open and heading towards me. Without anywhere to escape to, I stood there paralyzed with my eyes closed, and all I could do was pray, **"Jesus save us!"** Miraculously, as I stood still, I survived the earthquake and its devastating effects, unscathed.

These dreams confirmed for me that our journey on earth is dependent upon our listening to the word of God, and imitating Him and His followers as they lead us by their examples to salvation. When you are still and attuned to this voice, the words, ***"Follow me"***, will resound in your heart, not as a command, but as an invitation to enjoy the fullness of life. When you hear this voice, you will want to respond not because of human instinct, but because you know that following Christ will change you.

In the bible I read, "*Be still and know that I am God*" (Psalm 46:10). This bible quote is the voice I have come to hear and follow in my path of simplicity and humility. In my stillness, I stop and say, "Speak Lord for your servant is listening". Then I try to listen carefully for His voice. When you learn to listen for it, you recognize that the Lord is speaking to you with a gentle whisper, or, a still, small voice that enlightens your thoughts and puts a new idea directly and immediately into your mind. The Lord gives you a new perspective in which to view things. He puts new desires into your heart to arouse certain memories stored within your mind just when you need them the most. Martin Luther wrote: *"If the Holy Spirit should come when these thoughts are in your mind and begin to preach to your heart, giving you rich and enlightened thoughts, then give Him the honor, let your preconceived ideas go, be quiet and listen to Him who can talk better than you; and note what He proclaims and write it down."*

In time you will learn to recognize the Lord's voice and be able to distinguish it from all others that claim to be the Lord. Usually I know when the Lord is speaking to me because He fills me with the fruits of the Holy Spirit such as; love and peace, so that when I am studying, teaching or preparing a lesson, I am aware of the rich and enlightening thoughts that God sends me. As well, when I am counseling, I am always sensitive to the situation at hand as God directs me and I speak words of encouragement, peace, comfort and strength.

> *"Peace I leave with you; my peace I give you. I do not give to you as the world gives. Do not let your hearts be troubled and do not be afraid" (John 14:27). "And the peace of God, which transcends all understanding, will guard your hearts and your minds in Christ Jesus" (Philippians 4:6-7).*

The Lord also tells me how to carry on my daily responsibilities in my ministry work and with my charity and just as God provided Moses with the words he needed to speak to His people in Exodus (4:10-12), I'm sure you too have experienced a time in your life when you were talking to someone and all of a sudden the right thought came to you and suddenly you were able to explain something in a way you never thought you could. Well, this is the Lord speaking to you, revealing His wonderful, powerful and majestic ways of communication with you through the Holy Spirit. I believe He does this so that we will respond with praise, worship and a spirit of gratitude and when we feel God's love deep within our soul, then our natural response is to worship and love Him back. So whether you are listening to music or sitting outside admiring the beautiful cardinals, remember to let your soul be STILL and listen to the Lord as He speaks to your Heart in that still small voice!

REFLECTION: Take the scripture passage Psalm 46:10 and spend time with it.

"Be still and know that I am God". Repeat it silently, focus on the last word "God" and then listen with your heart. Continue with the passage.

"*Be still and know that I am*" Focus on the word "I am". Listen to what it is revealing to you.

"Be still and know", Let the word "know" fill you and listen to whatever it is you need to know.

"Be still", Stop from "doing" and "thinking". Now focus on the final word,

"Be". It is in our "being" that we begin to listen with our heart.

Excerpts from Chapter 12, Simple Contact with God, from Cris Smith's Spiritual Writings, "Let the Spirit Fly Wherever it Takes You."

Chapter 3

"Perfect Love Casts out Fear"
1 John 4:18

During my transformation, the Lord spoke to me through Scripture. For years I was afraid of giving of myself completely to the Lord. I believed that to do so would mean a sudden death or that some tragedy would befall on me or my family, as a way of testing my faith. I never shared this with anyone but He knew my heart was contaminated with fear, guilt, anger, and inferiority.

I guess it all stems back to my past. Back in the sixties as a young teenager, I hungered for an identity and found myself questioning my purpose in life. The feminist movement influenced my role as a woman with songs like, *"I am woman, hear me roar . . . ."* through, national advertisements and through the humanistic, care-free hippie lifestyle of love and peace which promoted an attitude of *"if it feels good, do it"*. I recall a beer commercial in particular that won national exposure for their multi-million dollar promotion that used the subliminal words, "I AM" to promote a positive self-image. I also recall hearing the words, 'I AM' again in a poem where the author used these words to explain the meaning of existence by writing, *"Yes, you are, I understand because **I am** too. Each of us exists separate and alone . . ."* you get the picture. Needless to say, at the time, I didn't know how sacrilegious this advertisement or the poem really was.

Then once again those same two words, 'I AM' were used in a movie entitled; 'THE BIBLE'. I must admit, the movie did inspire me to read the bible for a while, that is, until I got to the genealogy section. My relationship with Jesus was affected because of the identity crisis I experienced during these past years.

One night, I accompanied my husband to our church and joined him during the formation session he was taking. It was called RCIA (Rights for Christian Initiation for Adults), a program offered for adults who are not Catholic and who wish to convert to the Catholic Faith. The teaching that night was on scripture and the catechist explained how God will speak to us through the words found in the bible. I have to admit that after hearing this, I was inspired to read the Bible again. That night, I learned we are not supposed to read the bible like a book, since the bible is made up of many books. Instead, it was suggested we begin with the four gospels; Matthew, Mark, Luke and John. Then gradually continue with the rest of the New Testament which include the Psalms and the Proverbs, finishing off with the Old Testament. We learned that a passage from scripture should be read slowly at first, and then read again in order to meditate on the words and message that God wishes to speak to us. I began to do this every night before going to bed and one night as I turned to 1 John 4:18 and meditated on this passage. I immediately heard Him speak to me and say:

> *"There is no fear in love, but perfect love casts out fear because fear has to do with punishment, and so one who fears is not yet perfect in love."* 1 John 4:18

That night I felt as if the bible verse literally jumped off the page towards me and I knew it was the Lord helping me with this process.

Faith had become the anchor in my soul. Hope had assured me I had a purpose for living, a reason for praying because He was the source of my energy. By practicing the presence of God in my life I discovered the true meaning of peace and love. My journey towards finding my Jesus, strengthened my family and led us through many wonderful experiences together and with confidence I can say that today, "I AM" a living spirit created in the image of God. This road that I have been traveling on since that first major turning point in my life, almost 25 years ago, has had its trials and tribulations but in the midst of it all, it brought joy and happiness because without God in my life, I can honestly say I would not have survived the birth and death of my eighth child, Sara. It was during this time, that the Father Himself captured my heart in such a profound and gentle way and through the grace of life and the grace of death; my husband and I experienced His Love for us in a personal way.

Since then, I have never doubted my decision to follow that still small voice. I know that God is the 'I AM', I was searching for and that he never intended for me to be separated from Him or alone because "I sought the Lord, and He heard me, and delivered me from all my fears." Psalm 34:4

INVITATION: Perhaps you have a bible that has not been read for some time. If so, I invite you to open it randomly to any one of the gospels, psalms or proverbs. Begin to read until you feel the need to stop, either at the end of a verse, paragraph or story. Read it over slowly a second time. Is there any word or phrase that sticks out or seems to grab your attention? Focus on it as you read it slowly one last time. Then close your eyes, remain still and let the words speak to your heart. If you have a journal you may feel inspired to write. Eventually as you grow in the word through prayer and bible study you can open the bible to more chapters found in the New and Old Testament.

Excerpts taken from Chapter 2, The Reflection in the Mirror from Cris Smith's Spiritual writings in "Let the Spirit Fly Wherever It Takes You"

Chapter 4

Guide My Way

"Trust in the LORD with all your heart, And lean not on your own understanding; In all your ways acknowledge Him, And He shall direct your paths." Proverb 3:5-6

When I first read these words they seemed to be a little too profound for me to fully understand. It took the next few years for me to realize God was directing my path and guiding my steps in order to fulfill His will for my life. It all made sense in hindsight after my husband and I had became Salesian Cooperators. This Apostolate allowed us to serve God by witnessing to everyone we met, especially the young, through our words and our own deeds at home.

Albert Schweitzer, a theologian once said, *"Some people we meet or become acquainted with can make such a powerful impression on us, they never seem to leave us. In everyone's life, sometimes the inner fire goes out. It is then burst into flame by an encounter with another human being. We should all be thankful for these people who rekindle the inner spirit."*

God did this for me by bringing the Salesian Family into my life. Initially it began with Fr. Nino, our pastor who not only guided my husband during his conversion, but who administered the sacrament of reconciliation to me after 10 years. Then my husband and I were invited to attend our first Salesian Cooperator meeting that lead us to ministry work with youth.

Little did I know how many more spiritual people God would put into my path. Shortly after becoming a Salesian Cooperator, God sent two

Salesian priests to help Don and I in our spiritual process; Father Dave, a 6ft. 2in, bearded, Salesian Priest, who looked like Jesus, and Father Kelly, who can only be described as a jolly Santa Claus. Both these priests were instrumental in helping us become members of the Salesian Family. This in turn, opened many doors for us leading us to places we had never anticipated.

Being a Salesian Cooperator, providentially allowed me to connect with Fr. Bosio a 80 year old Salesian priest from New York. He was instrumental in sending me a few copies of a book called "He & I". I'll never forget the prophetic note he included with my package. It read;

> *"Thank you for your bubbly enthusiasm about the Lord Jesus and His book.*
> *"Let it Fly" wherever you detect God's hunger and thirst which is from the Spirit."*

That day marked the beginning of many more blessings, simply because we united with one of God's servants—Fr. Bosio. Never would I have imagined that years later these words would be the inspiration to the title of my spiritual writings.

Throughout my journey, God united me with many like-minded people who helped me along my path and while some stayed for only a season, the effects of those encounters will bear much fruit for years and years to come.

While each encounter was unique, I noticed a commonality in all of the people God sent to help me. They all shared the same insightfulness, wisdom, and independence that empowered me to do what was right and good through their teaching, correction and love. I realized that all this could not be done without their great capacity to be compassionate, sensitive, caring and giving of them selflessly which only confirmed for me the fact that these were godly people whose purpose in life was to love and serve the Lord.

Over the years, I have been blessed to know these people and witness first hand their genuine faith. Through their courage and support they taught me how to live up to my calling. I have come to realize that during our lifetime, brief encounters with these special messengers sent by God may seldom occur, but when they do, they bring meaning to one's work, helping us pay attention to areas in our lives that are most in need of spiritual direction, healing and love.

I first met Fr. Andrea, another charismatic priest, while he was here visiting Canada. We briefly met on, March 24, which just so happened to be the date of my wedding anniversary.

Seemingly three days earlier on March 21, Fr. Andrea was introduced to a woman named Rosanna, by a friend of hers named Laura Rubino. He was meeting Rosanna for the first time and like me, she too was a mother who suffered the loss of a child. Unknowingly to the both of us, this brief encounter would become a link to an incredible chain of events because what followed from these two separate and yet similar encounters with Fr. Andrea, would leave me to believe that it was Divine Intervention.

Fr. Andrea was instrumental in writing a book about Rosanna's son named Stephen, entitled "Stephen's Last Goal". The book gave a powerful account of Rosanna's son's battle with cancer, their family's journey of faith and hope and their testimony to God's love. Ironically, I too was suffering the loss of my eighth child, Sara, who lived only 26 days after being born. I first came across this book when a friend of mine pointed out that the pain Rosanna and her family endured during her trial with Stephen seemed to be similar to my story about Sara and that our similar experiences could bring so much healing to so many people.

I first realized that I had a connection with Rosanna when I noticed that the author of the book was none the other than Fr. Andrea, the same priest I had met on March 24 and that Rosanna had met three days earlier. That evening after reading half way through the book I began to put together pieces in this divine puzzle together. I remembered the book made reference to a woman named Laura Rubino, who joined Rosanna and her family in prayer at their home. This was my first sign. I knew that this was not happening by chance because Laura was also my good friend who initially insisted that I go see Fr. Andrea years earlier. Then I remembered as well, that Stephen was the young boy that Laura had called me about and asked me to pray for, especially during the 3-year period when Stephen was undergoing numerous operations. When Stephen passed away on March 11, 1992, my family attended a fundraiser dinner/dance and it was at that event that Laura introduced me to Stephen's parents but I had no idea that evening, that I would meet this woman, Rosanna again years later and share with her the pain and suffering of losing a child.

Through Stephen and his family, God blessed me with His presence and love and I felt Stephen's presence as I read the book, and as an afterthought I realized that Stephen was perhaps united with my Sara, in a mission of bringing faith, hope and love to us all. I called Laura that evening, to thank her for what she had done for me so long ago and I also felt compelled to contact Rosanna. It was at this point in our conversation that Rosanna and I discovered our connection with Fr. Andrea. We realized that meeting Fr. Andrea days apart from each other was not by chance since those dates were so significant to the both of us and what touched us deeply was the realization that both Sara and Stephen were conceived in the month of July.

Although we both began our journeys heading to different directions, our walk with God lead us to the same road that allowed us to meet one another on the same path. They say that nothing happens by chance and there are no such things as accidents when God is involved! God's enduring faithfulness, generosity and compassion brought us together to help and influence each other and bear witness to His love. Are there any people you can think of that do the same for you?

Excerpts taken from Chapter 10, God's Love in Action, from Cris Smith's Spiritual Writings in "Let the Spirit Fly Wherever It Takes You."

Chapter 5

Human Angels in Our Midst

Not to worry about things but to have a peace that goes beyond understanding, knowing that God will provide.

Ten months after the death of my daughter, Sara, God blessed my husband, Don and I once again with a daughter we named Stephanie. He filled us with such joy in the midst of our sorrow.

A few days after delivering Stephanie, I anxiously awaited the results from Stephanie's blood work that was sent to Sick Kids hospital the night before to confirm whether or not she carried any genetic anomalies like her sister Sara. I remember the initial shock I felt when the hospital staff told me they did this because they thought it was something I would want to have done, but I never once considered that there could be anything wrong with Stephanie, especially when I saw her beautiful face. That day, my good friend Maureen came to visit me to share Sunday's gospel reading. She had no idea how the Lord had used her to give me strength and to bring healing to my fears since I did not tell anyone about the blood tests. I tried to remain faithful and trust the Lord, but reliving this moment was just too much. All the strength, joy and peace I had been given during my pregnancy with Stephanie was slowly vanishing and being replaced with uncontrollable tears. Suddenly my peace turned into doubt and confusion as I waited for the results with my husband. Don tried to comfort me the best he could and told me that we would deal with whatever Stephanie's situation was, together. He reminded me that we had already discussed all the consequences that might occur before we made the decision to conceive again and that we agreed to trust and accept God's will for us. I agreed with him that we had come so far in this journey with Stephanie since we had conquered so many complications during my pregnancy already. All the complications that presented themselves started six months into my pregnancy when I had to be hospitalized for two weeks because I was hemorrhaging. Only one month later, I was back in the hospital where I remained for forty days until her birth. Then with only two weeks left into my pregnancy, it was determined that I would be induced. You cannot imagine the joy I felt in the anticipation of seeing my baby. As expected, a few hours later my daughter Stephanie was born and all was accepted with resignation as we felt that the hand of God had seen us through it all.

However, this unexpected turn of events which the hospital staff all seemed concerned about took me totally off guard. That evening seemed to get heavier as each hour passed. Since the results would take a few days, I tried to pray: "Please Lord tell me what is wrong because the waiting is unbearable." The unknown was resurrecting all these emotions of grief and sorrow that I had buried deep inside of me after Sara died, so I reacted by calling a good friend of mine named Mimma, who is a charismatic woman gifted with words of knowledge. I didn't know if she could tell me anything, but I knew that I needed to ask her to pray for me. She immediately prayed with me and reassured me that God was with me and that I was to trust Him in faith. Her words allowed me to rest for a while, but inside, I still longed for the Lord to give me a sign, any sign that would tell me everything was going to be okay. The next morning when I opened my eyes, I found my special friend Maureen, standing next to my bed. I immediately thanked God for sending her to me because more than anything else, I needed my mother to be with me during this time and since my mother passed away the same year I was expecting Stephanie, Maureen was filling my mother's shoes and bringing me her love and comfort as she had done many times before.

That morning when I needed her most, Maureen had come to see me rather apologetically, because it was still so early. She had come directly from mass because she felt that the Lord had a word for me from Philippians 4:6.

> *"Do not be anxious about anything, but in everything, by prayer and petition, with thanksgiving, present your request to God. And the peace of God, which transcends all understanding, will guard your hearts and your minds in Christ Jesus." (Phil 4:6)*

I could not bring myself to telling her that I was anxious about the next 48 hours, which would reveal either good or bad news about Stephanie. Not wanting to give her any reason to worry, I never let on how much I needed to see her and how that scripture passage would be God's sign for me and my confirmation that everything would be okay. Through His word I had been healed. The burden had been lifted and I could soar once again with My Lord who promised that He would never "leave me nor forsake me". (Heb. 13:5)

I walked into the nursery that morning with a renewed sense of peace and calm that the Lord had given me. The doctors and nurses were still apprehensive regarding the outcome of the test results but I did not let this affect me. Instead, through the kindness of the doctor who shared a few moments of his time with me, I was given the opportunity to witness to him. I remember with much surprise the comment he made to me before leaving. He said, *"Tomorrow I will come back and talk some more with you because I want to get to know your Jesus!"* I smiled because his Jesus was the same Jesus I knew and yet he felt that I knew Him better.

The next day the doctor still could not tell me anything and left hoping to bring good news the following day. The nurses could not wait that long so they used their influence to speed up the process. With great jubilation that day at the hour of the Lord's Divine Mercy, 3:00 p.m. the nurse in charge walked in and with a big smile on her face told me what God had already impressed upon my heart. *"Stephanie is a beautiful, healthy, baby girl, with no genetic disorders of any kind."* I smiled and thanked God for revealing His great love for me giving me peace in my heart through His Divine Mercy. Praise God!

Reflection: Who are the human angels that have come into your life's journey? When anxiety hits, who is it that fills your heart with peace, a peace that goes beyond understanding? Is it a doctor, a nurse, a friend, a parent, a spouse, a teacher, a child, or maybe even a stranger? Who has God sent or sending you to right now, who is in need of a human angel to help them hear a message of love?

Chapter 6

Nightly Dramas

Sometimes God speaks to me in my dreams through what I call nightly parables that help me with my transformation. Most of the time, my dreams tell me something about who I am, and how I deal with everyday life experiences. Not all my dreams are good ones, some are filled with joy while others are filled with fears and sadness, but almost always my dreams are symbolic to me. Understanding our personal dreams can help us deal with issues in our daily lives or change our lives for the better. Dreams from God can guide us and direct our faith so paying attention to the message and learning how to interpret our dreams is important since our dreams are another way of listening to God.

> *"For in one way God may speak and in a second, but one does not regard it. In a dream, a vision of the night, when deep sleep falls on men; while they slumber on the bed, then He opens the ear of men and seals their instruction." (Job 33:14)*

In the bible, God used many special servants to deliver His message through a dream. He used Gabriel, the Archangel, who appeared to Joseph three times in the bible. First, to tell him that he should take Mary to be his wife and name her son Jesus.

> *"But when he had considered this, behold, an angel of the Lord appeared to him in a dream, saying, "Joseph, son of David, do not*

> be afraid to take Mary as your wife; for the Child who has been conceived in her is of the Holy Spirit". (Matthew 1:20)

The second time, to warn him that King Herod was going to come and kill the baby Jesus.

Now when they had gone, behold, an angel of the Lord appeared to Joseph in a dream and said, "Get up! Take the Child and His mother and flee to Egypt, and remain there until I tell you; for Herod is going to search for the Child to destroy Him." (Matthew 2:13) and then the third time to tell him that Herod was dead and that it was safe to return to Israel.

> *"After Herod died, an angel of the Lord appeared in a dream to Joseph in Egypt* [20] *and said, "Get up, take the child and his mother and go to the land of Israel, for those who were trying to take the child's life are dead." (Matthew 2:19)*

What would the world be like today, if saints like St. Joseph, St. Paul, and Don Bosco had ignored their dreams or visions of the night?

Dreams happen for many reasons: to announce, confirm, warn, protect, guard, rule or guide us. In an attempt to understand my dreams, I realized dreams can reveal something from the depth of us all and I knew that if I viewed the world with the eyes of Jesus, and followed a few basic rules, then I would learn how to interpret the message of my dreams. The first rule was to establish that God could speak through dreams. The second was to keep a written record of my dreams. Thirdly, I was blessed to have a spiritual guide or friend with whom I could talk over these strange and wonderful visitations of the night and lastly I prayed to God for help in understanding my dreams.

My Transforming Dream, I found myself standing in front of a wall in my mother's house. The wall began to transform itself and it became a fountain with flowing water pouring out, drawing me closer to it. As I watched, I suddenly sensed the presence of Jesus. I heard Him speak to me. He said, *"I will give you 3 wishes. Ask what you want and I will give it you."* Without any hesitation, I replied, *"I just want health and happiness and that's all."* I woke up remembering the dream and shared it with my family. Not much thought went into it after that but I could not deny the wonderful sense of peace I had experienced.

Dream Journal Entry: In this dream from 1989—I was in my third year of walking with the Lord. I began to realize how God was allowing me to remember my dreams with such vividness and clarity. This indicated to me that the events or warnings forecasted by my dreams must be very important. In fact, it would not be until 1994, after doing research for one of the Salesian Cooperator magazine, that I was writing for, that I fully understood the meaning of dreams. I realized that not only was God speaking to me through them but it was also a way of listening to God. I was so excited that I decided it was time to start a dream journal to record the ones that touched me the most during the past three years, especially those that involved my spiritual journey in unity with my family. I knew the Lord would approve of this and would help me to discern what He was trying to teach me through my dreams and visions. Initially, I could not fully understand my dreams and then with time I began to figure out parts and sections of my dreams. Then I found myself examining past dreams, months or even years later and I discovered the Lord was giving me a deeper and fuller meaning behind those same dreams.

For example, my dream of 'three wishes' I believed was self-explanatory. I wanted 'Health' and 'Happiness'. The only question that remained in my mind was what that third wish should be. When I read what I had recorded in my dream journal, three years ago, I discovered that perhaps there could be a deeper meaning behind the symbols of the three wishes or the fountain and the water. My confirmation came when I read the biographical memoirs of Don Bosco Vol. 1. Page 99 in which he quotes Sirach 30: 14-16

> "Better a poor man strong and robust than a rich man with wasted frame. More precious than gold is health and well-being, contentment of spirit than coral. No treasure greater than a **healthy** body; no **happiness** than a joyful heart."

Unknowingly, the unspoken word was being given to me through Scripture and I learned then that the Lord was teaching me what I needed to know gently, within His own timing as if to signify that a part of me still needed to grow spiritually.

As a confirmation of my dream, I discovered a program called the 3H Club. It encouraged everyone in becoming a member by simply reciting 3 Hail Marys, so that God would grant us the graces needed to acquire

Health, Happiness and Holiness. And so my third wish, was going to be holiness in order to continue my journey of faith.

The Lord waited for me to reach a level of spiritual growth before He could further explain to me the full meaning behind the fountain and the water, which had still remained a mystery.

> *"The water that I shall give will become a fountain of living water springing up into everlasting life." (John 4:14)*

Finally I knew what the fountain and water symbolized in my dream. In John 4:14, Jesus revealed to me that the way to Health, Happiness and Holiness was through Him, Our Lord Jesus Christ, who invites us to drink from this life-giving fountain and experience success in our spiritual journey.

Ten years later Jesus continues to teach me by inviting me to the waters of everlasting life.

JOURNAL ENTRY—March 6, 1996: Feeling frustrated and confused about certain things and people in my life, I asked the Lord to help me. While writing in my journal I asked Him for spiritual awareness and direction and wrote out the words, "Speak, Lord. I'm listening". As I listened with the ears of my heart I began to write these words down and felt strongly that Jesus was the one speaking to me. This is what I wrote,

> *"I have been speaking but you haven't been listening. You are not sure of many things. You drift like a ship at sea with no navigator. You are the navigator, you steer but you also need to know by listening where you are to go. The ocean is so vast. How can you go anywhere without me? You would be lost indeed. With me you can safely set out blindly—and yet—spiritually aware of the path I lead you on. There will be moments when the waters become enraged. A storm brews. A hurricane hits. All these are like the stirring within your soul. Remain in me. Fear not, for it all will subside and calm will replace it. My grace, remember, is sufficient to get you through. You are to take passengers on this journey. Many need to travel short distances; many need to travel further. While you navigate, you look out for them and provide according to your means for their well being. I have placed them there. Take care of them*

and when it is time for them to disembark, you will know. You will warn them ahead of time. Your task is to help them arrive. In unity you can fight the storms much better. Remember, correct, teach, and love. Pray to St. Christopher, he will help you get these people across to safety. Remember when the weight is too heavy on your shoulder that I am there. I love you. I love you too, my precious lord. Then go forth strengthened in my love. Lord, shower me in your love. Bathe me in your light. Drown me in your life. "You can do this every day through my Eucharist."

Recording and reflecting on our nightly dramas can help us with listening because they may just draw us closer to the Spirit that lives inside our heart. My journal writing helps me connect and remember just like albums and scrap books. A dream journal or just simply journal writing can become a powerful tool that helps to listen to that transforming message that can be heard deep within our soul.

(See the end of the book for instructions on how to start a dream journal).

Excerpts taken from Chapter 3, Journey of Faith from Cris Smith's Spiritual Writings, "Let the Spirit Fly Wherever It Takes You."

Chapter 7

Love Language

The more we see how much we are connected to each other and how much we need to love each other, the better we can hear God.

A TRIBUTE TO CONCETTA

Concetta was the type of person who touched many hearts because of who she was and during our 15 years of friendship, she made a difference in my life.

I met Concetta through her daughter named Rose, who worked as a secretary at our local community high school, Monsignor Johnson High School. I first met Rose in March during the feast of St. Joseph. She came over to my house for a visit and brought zepoli for dessert, a traditional Italian pastry usually made during this time of year to honour St. Joseph. During our visit, I remember Rose telling me that on December 8th the feast of the Immaculate Conception, her brother who was only 26 years old at the time, had been diagnosed with prostate cancer. That day, Rose and I prayed together and every day thereafter. I also made sure to ask my prayer warriors to also include Vince in their daily prayers. Four months later, on July 16th my family and I attended a wedding at St. David's parish in Maple. After the ceremony we went to visit with Rose, since she lived close to the church. I felt blessed the moment I walked into her home as I finally had the opportunity to meet her whole family. I was first introduced to her brother, Vince, a talented artist who was dying in the prime of his life, her dad, Nick, a pillar of strength, and Anna, her older 50 year old sister who was born developmentally delayed. Even though Anna's disability could not allow her to communicate with us verbally, her joyful smile, hand gestures and facial expressions told us that we were welcomed. That was also the day I met Rose's mother, Concetta. I will never forget my first impression of her. I was drawn to her motherly love as she served her family and friends with gentleness and humility.

The years followed and our relationship deepened as we continued to pray together, and share many stories. Concetta's life stories helped further strengthen me, spiritually. She was a witness to me of what it meant to be not only a Godly woman, but also a mother and a wife.

Throughout the years, Concetta and her husband, Nick, made it a point to visit my family at least twice a year. They always came bearing gifts that providentially helped the needs of our large family both materially and spiritually. Her words of encouragement and support were always grace-filled. I still remember how her presence during my time of grief over the loss of my daughter Sara, brought me strength knowing that like her, I too would find the strength to carry on.

Sadly enough, Concetta's son Vince, passed away on February 11th. My daughter Sara, also died on the 11th day in May and Concetta passed away on January 11th. the feast of the Baptism of Our Lord. There is no doubt that Concetta was special to the Lord and like Mother Mary emulated many of her qualities, especially those that help God's children come closer to Jesus.

Concetta opened her heart to me and shared her life stories, her dreams and visions with me. Two stories in particular I would like to share with you still remain strong in my memory. The first deals with her humility, the second, her salvation.

The first story she shared with me was during the time when she was a young woman. She shared how in those days school just wasn't as important as helping out the family and because of this she never had the opportunity to go to school like many of her other friends. She looks sad as she tells me that she regrets the fact that she never learned how to read and write. She tells me about her first year of marriage to Nick. Her precious Nick was drafted and needs to go away to serve in the army. Knowing that her relationship for the next year is going to be long and lonely she resigns herself with the knowledge that they can continue to remain connected through the mail. Being that this would be the most feasible form of communication she managed to find the strength to ask any one of her neighbors who were younger and willing to write a letter for her. With humility Concetta takes her love letters from Nick and overcoming her embarrassment she manages to get them read.

In response she also finds the courage to dictate a response knowing that he would hear her true message in between the words she allowed herself to share with the letter writer.

Many an unspoken word can still communicate between the lines and received with love becoming a language of its own. This can only be done when a heart carries a spirit of giving and humility, qualities that Concetta possessed.

The second story is actually a dream. In this dream Concetta sees herself holding her daughter Rose's hand, who at the time was only 5 years old. Together they walked to church. She stops to reflect back for a moment and tells me how she remembers actually doing this every morning with her little Rose. Even when the weather was bitterly cold they would walk together hand in hand to church for morning mass, before she went to work. Sometimes, they would stop at a nearby store just to warm up a little. Then she continues to tell me about her dream. She says that she vividly sees herself walking through the parish doors, entering the church, sitting in a pew, singing, praying, and receiving the Eucharist. At the end of mass, everyone leaves. She proceeds down the aisle also to leave the church, but something odd is happening. She said that she found herself staring at the crucifix of Jesus. The cross that normally stood at the altar was now standing at the doorway and she immediately understands the meaning of this. She said that with God's grace she understood that Jesus was inviting her to take the crucifixion with her into the world. She continued to explain that by exiting through the church doors into the world outside, she was being called to live everyday with a new confidence and faith knowing that her strength will come from embracing her crosses and uniting her suffering with Jesus.

The most amazing part of this story is that, not only did this dream become life changing for her as she shared with me this understanding of embracing the cross, but it also continued to open the doors as she witnessed God's miracles in her life. One of her greatest miracles that she received shortly after this dream was her ability to read scripture. Concetta said that God miraculously answered her prayers and allowed her to be able to read the bible along with all her prayers. This brought her so much joy.

Throughout her life Concetta could be counted on as a powerful prayer warrior.

Even in her dying moments Concetta continued to share her prayers and love with everyone. Her last lesson to me happened last week while I was visiting with her at the hospital. It was a lesson on living in PEACE and surrendering to God's will. When my husband and I entered her room, Nick came over and welcomed us. Concetta immediately recognized me. Her joy, her smile and her words of praise for me, my husband and my family erased all of the world's concerns that I had been carrying for the past few weeks. She replaced it with her peace. Can you imagine that . . . in the midst of her suffering she was sharing her PEACE with me!

I think it is so fitting that my friendship with Concetta and her family began years ago over a shared meal—a meal filled with a spirit of rejoicing and celebration. I am so grateful to God that He blessed us with one last visit and that once again we were able to share a meal—this meal being the body of Christ—and it was shared in the same spirit of rejoicing.

I will never forget her last words to me. She said, Tu sei un profumo del paradise which means "***You are a heavenly fragrance from heaven.***" No one has ever said that to me and I knew that was a special farewell gift she had given me. I left the room knowing that I would never see her alive in the flesh again, but felt I would now have another great saint in heaven who would continue to look out for my needs as she did for so long. More importantly, I will have a friend in heaven who will help me as I journey here on earth to learn to embrace my cross with humility, in complete trust and surrender to His will.

My husband and I left that room filled with the grace of life and the grace of death and peace . . . HIS PEACE that surpasses all understanding. May she rest in peace.

REFLECTION: Is there someone in your life that you can pay tribute to? Someone who has blessed you with the grace of life or the grace of death?

Write about them in your journal and feel the connection you have with them. Perhaps they no longer live with you because of separation or death. This can leave us with feelings of unresolved loss, grief and a need to hear and feel close again. Or perhaps we are at peace and we have made a connection that continues to live on in our hearts. What is it that keeps them close to your heart? Is it something they shared with you? Is it something you shared with them as they listened to what you said or did? Aside from the fact that writing about it can bring much healing and continued joy, it can also continue to keep the lines of communication open with this person by remaining connected with them in spirit.

Chapter 8

Soul Imprints

In the wonder of creation and nature, we can see God and understand God's love better. God keeps pouring His blessings on all his children and as a sign of hope for my family He spoke to us through His creations.

This incredible manifestation of God's beauty actually began the night my sons performed at our local parish for a confirmation kickoff. Over 300 parents, sponsors and students were present. That evening, I felt souls were being touched and that God was pleased with us. I shared this with my sons and they chuckled because according to them, I sometimes get a little carried away with my spiritual excitement. Well . . . . you can imagine my joy when the very next day, God spoke to me and sent me a sign that surprised even my sons.

Five of my six sons who were working on a new song all morning came out of the studio and were all standing in the kitchen at the same time. It was one of my sons who saw the first sign and drew our attention to it. A beautiful red cardinal came and perched itself on the deck ledge and we all thought it was awesome . . . but then a second cardinal joined the first, and while flying around, a third cardinal approached, then a fourth landed gracefully inches away on the top ledge of the gate, and finally encircling them all, came a fifth, sixth, and seventh cardinal. It can only be described as a heavenly sight for sure! Would you believe SEVEN . . . not one or two but SEVEN beautiful, RED cardinals came to rest on my deck that day!

Of course my son's teased me because I was just screeching with excitement and telling them that this was a SIGN from God of good things to come if we continue to help and witness to others. Their response of course was not as expressive as mine and they commented by saying "Well mom, then this sign must include us as well since we saw it too!"

That day, I saw all my sons staring in awe at these beautiful cardinals that just 'happened' to come at that 'precise' moment. This moment was brief but it made us all STOP what we were doing and it drew us in, like a spellbound audience watching a performance where the cardinals' melodic movements expressed and resonated a spirit of unity and love.

I believe God used a brief moment like this to get our attention and make us stop and listen. When we come together and share the beauty and wonder of creation and nature, we can see the Spirit we carry inside our hearts that can make a difference in the lives of others. Experiencing brief moments like this one can leave a lasting imprint on our souls forever. So, if a beautiful cardinal comes your way . . . STOP, take a moment and experience the JOY it brings and then go out and do the same for someone else.

REFLECTION: Think of an animal that has shown up in your life? Was it a coincidence? Perhaps the animal was there performing its usual ecological function but did it's appearance increase your sense of awareness or healing even for a moment? Did it move you to feel a sense of peace, or connection with, making the encounter seem almost mystical? Is there an animal or pet that still continues to bring you joy, peace, protection, security manifesting it's powerful message that speaks directly to your heart?

Chapter 9

The Impact of Giving

God will occasionally speak to us through the actions and/or words of other people. We need to be open to Him doing this and discern what is being communicated and from where it originates.

The other day as I stood waiting in line at the grocery checkout, an older gentleman, possibly in his eighties, stood behind me holding on to his 3 grocery items. I quickly made room for him on the counter so that he could rest his items. He nodded in appreciation as we exchanged smiles. Then just before the cashier finished punching in my last item, I felt the Lord telling me to pay for this gentleman's items too. He was holding a $20.00 bill in his hand so my eyes and mind knew that he had the money but my Spirit was prompting me to do it anyway. As my last item was being punched in, I motioned the cashier and told her to punch in this man's items too. The elderly man quickly told the cashier that those items were his, and that she was making a mistake. I told him I knew that and that I was going to pay for them. He repeated what I said thinking that he may have misunderstood what he had heard. So, I said it again and added that the Lord told me to do it so I wanted to pay for them. He was so grateful and responded by saying that he too believed in the Lord. He stood there speechless, looking at me and then managed to say thank you again as he moved towards me to give me a kiss on my cheek. He was so cute . . . I kissed him back.

He had tears in his eyes as he leaned in to tell me quietly that he had lost his wife 2 months ago. I looked at him and without hesitation I reassured him that this gesture of love was no doubt coming from her. I told him God loved him and that our loved ones are always with us in Spirit. I told him that I too lost a loved one, my daughter and that even though it was 8 years ago, I still felt her presence in Spirit. We chatted a bit and I told him about my family and raising 8 kids. I mentioned to him that when it is my time to go to heaven, my desire would be to leave this earth together with my husband, but I told him that my husband always reminds me that it would be too painful for the children if we both left them and so one of us would have to stay behind a little while longer for the sake of them.

At this, he responded by telling me that he has 2 daughters. Imagine—they are probably older than me?

He also told me that he was 88 years old. God bless him! I noticed after he left that there was a younger man with him that must have been his driver.

As unbelievable as it may seem that a stranger would do something like this, I know the Lord used me that day to connect not only with this elderly gentleman, but with the cashier as well, who needless to say was surprised and touched by this whole experience too. I for one, was on a high all day just thinking about the events of the day and I even shared this story with many people. It felt good to give and share. Maybe the Lord wanted to give him a reason to live and used me as his instrument to convey His message.

I can't tell you how good it made me feel. I was being used to let this man know that his wife still loved him and was still looking out for him. What if he was losing hope and wondering if he could make it without her. Who knows, maybe I was an answer to his prayer.

The moral of this story is keep listening with your heart when the Lord is calling you to give. Be open to how, where, when and why the Lord wishes to speak to you.

Never underestimate the impact you can have on others by your GIVING.

Chapter 10

Out of the Mouth of a Child

The ability to listen is a priceless skill. It involves paying attention to what others say and feel, and treating each person with dignity and respect. If we really listen to our children there are times when "out of the mouth of a child" some very profound and insightful thoughts can be communicated to us. This is exactly what happened to me one day as my son David yelled out with the kind of excitement that can only be expected from a small child who has just created a masterpiece.

"Mommy look! Look at what I drawed!"
"Oh what is it?" I replied.
"This is a tree and the branches."
"OH and what are all these 'F' letters on the top of the tree? I asked.
"Those are the seeds."
"Why did you draw this?"
"I don't know."

I, on the other hand, knew exactly what just transpired. This picture was God's way of using my son, David, a four year old, to confirm what I had just finished writing for our next Salesian Cooperators' Magazine. Simultaneously, as I sat pensively writing the first three paragraphs of my editor's note and wondering if this was the direction I should take in regards to our theme on "Friendship", David, unknowingly, had drawn exactly that which I had written.

This is what I wrote as he drew: ***"Looking back to my younger years as a teenager, I recall my participation in a speech-writing contest. My***

topic revolved on the subject of 'Friendship'. *My opening lines (which are the only words I can remember to this day) were:*

> "Friendship is like a tree,
> Just like a tree has many branches and leaves,
> So we too can have many friends.

I couldn't believe my eyes! I prayed to the Holy Spirit to guide me, as I always do before writing but never had I received such a wonderful confirmation of His guidance and presence as the one He sent me this day, especially from the mouth of a child.

I must admit that my husband is better at listening than I am. My problem is that I try to anticipate what the children will say or do, and then quickly react. However, with a family as large as mine, I have mastered the technique of listening to three or four people talking while talking on the phone all at the same time. As crazy as this may sound, there have been two crucial times during each day in which my listening skills were valued . . . after school and during bedtime. This is when my children shared with me their feelings, thoughts, dreams and fantasies.

Automatically, after school, my children would share with me their frustrations of the day and I listened as they told me their excuses for not bringing home their homework, the reasons for their detentions, being late for school or warning me about the possibility of the principal calling me. Then every so often I got to share in their joys too with something that happened at school or with their friends. Bedtime sharing varied according to age. The younger ones shared their prayers and got into the most philosophical talks you could imagine, anything to avoid switching off the lights and going to sleep.

The older ones instead enjoyed being invited to have a cup of tea with their mom and dad and stayed up to ask questions or discuss movies they recently watched or just talk about things that happen in school. In fact, one year my older sons watched a movie called **"Stigmata"** and they had a lot of questions about it. I had not seen the movie myself so I just explained to them what the word "stigmata' really meant in our faith compared to the Hollywood version.

As my sons got older, I noticed that they asked a lot of questions regarding spiritual matters. They were revealing their hunger to understand. This held true especially when they had a strange dream or vision. We enjoyed hearing the stories of our children's nightly visions. My eldest once had a visit from a little girl who stood smiling next to his bedside. We all listened to the details while trying to discern the meaning. Then we chuckled at how one son gets awakened by his brother because of his sleepwalking or talking in his sleep.

I'll never forget the revelation we all received one morning when I discovered something horrible hidden in one of the framed pictures they had hanging in their bedroom. I innocently sat in front of it (I was 8 months pregnant with our 8th) while trying to get my oldest son Jeff to wake up. I looked once again at the picture that we all had looked at for months without any thought other than it was a beautiful picture of a red electric Gibson Guitar. It was useful to have up there because in one corner of the picture a series of panatonics scales were outlined for reference. That same corner was shaped in the form of a mountain with a path that led from the base of the guitar to the top of this mountain and the path was made up of hundreds of people walking up towards it. It also looked like on the very tip of the mountain there was a ray of light that shone down on the crowd. It all looked innocent enough until this particular morning. I sat there staring as I had dozens of times before when all of the sudden I saw the picture in its true form. The light was in fact an eye, the mountain was a head, the tip of the mountain were horns attached to this demonic looking head, and the crowd of people on the path were in fact its arms stretched around the guitar representing power and possession. I was so aghast at this horrific sight that I yelled, and, of course, made every one aware of what I had just discovered hidden in this picture.

Needless to say, this reinforced my teachings that everything carries a spirit and that we are to be very careful as to what we allow into our homes. The evil one will always find a way of disguising himself in an effort to enter not only into our homes but eventually our souls. The picture was removed. The children understood, and to be understood is very satisfying especially if one is a parent.

As parents we are given the gift to understand our babies' needs. Children going through puberty are emotional and can't understand their own feelings. As parents, during this stage of their development, we need to go into overtime in our understanding of them. Older siblings, I can tell you from experience, can at times make it worse because they are quick to make fun of them. Being open to others, despite the day's busy routine, helps teach our children about the importance of sharing our Christian values through communication.

My children know that when I communicate with certain spiritual friends, we are praying or talking about God. We do not gossip or have vulgar and obscene conversations. Hopefully by our example they too will be able to make themselves available to others. One day I questioned Donny as to why he was giving his friend so much of his time when he had already spent hours with him during a sleep over. His reply was **"Hey, Mom, he's my brother!"** Need I say more?

Parenting, even under the best of circumstances, can be a difficult job, but when we carry a spirit of joy we can find the resources necessary for meeting the challenges. One resource is our own special gifts. We can comfort a person who feels hurt. We, can relate to children of all ages and we can communicate love and understanding. We as parents need to discover our own unique gifts, and use them to the fullest. Secondly, we need to be open to the gift of humbly listening with and to the heart of a child.

REFLECTION: We spend the first decade of our life looking at the world through the eyes of our parents. What is the light you wish to share that you wish to bring to and call forth in others? There is something burning inside of you which you know would, if ever fully released and fully expressed make your life and the life of others better? What is it? Joyfulness? Burning Bliss? Do not force this but allow it to create itself.

Excerpts taken from Chapter 11, "Parenting with a Spirit of Joy," from Cris Smith's Spiritual Writings, "Let the Spirit Fly, Whereever it Takes You."

Chapter 11

A Spirit Filled Moment

*Be open to how, where, when and
why the Lord wishes to speak to you.*

God will occasionally speak to us through inspiration. We need to be open to when it happens and discern what is being communicated and from where it originates.

It was June 9, 1995 and Sunday mass had just ended. As I made my way out of the church I could not help but notice a young man who still remained praying in the back pew. His head was hung low and his hands were cupped together in prayer. At first I thought I recognized him but realizing my mistake, I simply moved on to catch up to my two younger sons who were already out the front doors.

Finally catching up to them and taking a hold of their hands we began to make our way towards our parked car which was in the school yard next to the church. To my surprise, this same young man who moments earlier was praying in the church was now walking in our direction. His pace was a lot slower and he seemed to be in deep thought. I, on the other hand had two squirming children trying to get away from me and all I could think of was getting them into the car and making my way home. Suddenly, without any warning, I heard this voice in my head that said, "She will be fine. Tell him." I pretended to ignore it but it was very strong and my eyes quickly drew upon this man who was now moving closer to me. I could see that he had a look of despair and pain on his face. Then it happened again and this time I heard, "Do not fear, she will be fine". With it came this strong urge that this message was for this young distraught man. I simply continued walking straight towards my car while he turned to the left of me and went up a small flight of stairs. We separated going in two different directions, so I let this leading of the spirit go. I got the kids in the car, put the keys in the ignition and then it happened . . . again! This time the message was loud and clear and with more urgency, "Go tell him". I thought to myself, "Oh Lord" . . . "Then give me a sign" I asked. Then it happened. Right in front of me, was this man in the parking lot heading towards his car which happened to be the only other car left in the parking lot next to mine. At this point I got out of my car and stopped him in his tracks. I said "I'm probably going to make a fool of myself, but I heard something and I don't know if it means anything." I told him what I heard, "She'll be fine." He looked at me and responded by saying, "that is something" and then kept very still. I could tell that he believed me because he looked surprised and in awe with God that He would send this message to him, probably an answer to something he was praying for. I told him that the second time, I heard." *Do not fear, she'll be fine.*" Once again he nodded his head and said, *"That is something! Thank you."* I quickly left him and went back to my car as he walked towards his. I could tell that he was touched by this. I watched him as he sat in his car without turning on the ignition, stared out his window for a second and then put his face into his cupped hands. I left the parking lot as quickly as I could, realizing that something powerful had just happened and while I am driving off I hear, *"Marie, pray for her".* It was a strong request which I agreed to respond to in prayer. So I decided to pray for this young man and this woman named Marie whoever she was. That evening I shared this experience with my family and praised God for using me as his instrument of peace. However the story does not end here.

Two months later while I am taking my daughter to an evening church program, I am approached by another parent who is also dropping off his daughter. He approaches me and tells me that he recognizes me as the lady who spoke to him that morning in the parking lot. He goes on to tell me that it was his daughter whom he was praying for with all his heart on that particular Sunday morning. He introduces himself and his daughter to me and tells me once again that he has not forgotten what I did for him that day in the parking lot. He shares with me the agonizing pain he experienced when his daughter was taken away from him and out of the country by his ex-wife. Thinking he would never see her again and seeing no way of fighting for custody he prayed on that particular day for a sign that his daughter would be safe and that she would be returned to him. He told me that when I approached him and delivered a message that was so direct and to the point that he knew God had sent a complete stranger to answer his prayers. He knew that God was listening to him and giving him the strength to not give up in the hopes of finding his daughter. Without telling him that I had been praying for Marie and thinking that perhaps this was his daughter's name I asked him who Marie was. He told me that is his ex-wife's name was Marie. Marie was the women I was praying for all this time. Praise God, for not only did God use me to hear and share this powerful message with this man but He also inspired me to pray for Marie, a woman who needed a transformation of heart to see that returning her daughter back to ex-husband and giving him full custody was the right thing to do. What a confirmation this was of God's power and love speaking directly through others.

The story still continues to bear fruit even six years later. Once again, as I am walking towards the church, I encountered a man who greeted me. He was alone and I had my daughter, Stephanie with me. He overheard me calling her and he smiled. We made small talk at first and then I remembered that it was the same man with whom I shared that grace filled moment with in the parking lot years ago. He told me that he often thinks of that day and that he felt compelled to write the message down upon his return home so as not to forget it and shared this message with his family who were also convinced that God had spoken to them all. With renewed hope this man and his child were reunited. I agreed with him that this was truly a spirit filled moment in both our lives

REFLECTION: See what you are doing in a new way. See every moment and situation as an opportunity to be healing. Instead of being a healer decide simply to be healing.

How have you been called to be a bringer of light? What are your gifts and talents? Are you an encourager, or is someone encouraging you, making you happy which in turn allows you to make others happy?

Who you really are, is the very light you are seeking to bring to others. There is no brighter light in the universe than the light of your being. So let your light shine! How do you shine the light of your being?

Chapter 12

Treasured Gifts

It seemed that the Lord heard my prayers and He was about to reveal to me how I was to learn and teach the meaning of living the sacrament of the present moment, through the people who had been given 'time' sentences due to their terminal illnesses. My family was being called to listen and to prepare ourselves to personally meet these souls and their families.

I became acquainted to a lady, named Enza, who was 26 years old and who only had a few months to live. She was diagnosed with cancer during the pregnancy of her first child and sadly, left behind a beautiful 8th month old child named Sara. Enza was a beautiful woman, so young, so pretty with a beautiful smile that radiated right through you and even though we met at the hospital for the first time, somehow I felt we had known each other for years.

One month later, on March 10, 1994, Enza passed away. As I reflected on this spiritual journey, I tried to understand what my mission was with this young soul. My relationship with Enza lasted only two months, and yet something about her touched me spiritually. I asked God; why He would allow her to come into my life, allow me to love her only to then take her away so soon. God's answer became more evident to me a few months later, after personally meeting a young man named Vince. Vince was 25 years old and was also diagnosed with cancer. I realized that God wanted me to love and serve Him, by loving and serving his children and that God used Enza as his instrument to help prepare me for my next mission with Vince.

On April 1994, a few weeks after Enza's death, I was praying for Vince. Vince was a young man who was diagnosed with advanced prostate cancer and who had been given only 6 weeks to live. Vince was young, intelligent, and an artist who had so much to live for but it was evident that he was angry at the hand life had dealt him. This left me feeling a little unsure as to how far I would be able to talk to Vince about God and help him know that he was loved. During one of our conversations, I even shared with Vince the importance of acknowledging his Guardian Angel and invoking his aid.

Polite as he was with me on the phone, I sensed that he wasn't quite opening up fully to me about God and feeling loved. I faithfully continued to call him but at times, I have to be honest, I felt a little discouraged and even thought of giving up but then the most amazing thing happened.

The Lord showed me that Vince needed to talk and gave me the inspiration I needed to keep on finding a way to reach him. One day shortly after meeting Vince, I found something that I had lost many years ago. After having searched for it for some time, I eventually gave up on the hopes of finding it until that day, thirteen years later, when miraculously out of nowhere, I found my tiny, gold, guardian-angel medal that I received at baptism and that was very special to me. This happened to be that day when I was straightening out the covers on my bed and I heard something fall to the ground. Automatically I looked down towards my feet and there sitting on the floor before my very eyes, was my guardian-angel medal that I had lost thirteen years ago. It was as if it had fallen straight down from heaven! I picked it up in disbelief, only to be reassured by the small dent on the right side, that it was indeed my medal. I suddenly thought of Vince and I knew I had to share this with him so that he would know that angels are real and that we should acknowledge their presence because they are a gift from God to be treasured.

Inspired by this sign, I wrote Vince a note, sharing everything that had happened and attached my gold guardian-angel medal to it. I told him that I was lending it to him for as long as he needed it. I invited him to look at it every time he felt like giving up so that it would remind him of the powerful angels God surrounded him with, especially the Archangels.

A few weeks later, Rose, Vince's sister, tells me something her brother had said shortly after this transformation. The memory was sparked by the homily she had just heard at the Sunday Mass. She remembered Vince saying to her one day, in one of his mellow moods, how he felt that it was his *"time to retire."* It was as if he intuitively knew it was time. She asked me to pray for a word of knowledge that morning while I attended Mass. I agreed to pray and offered the Mass for Vince. After receiving communion I knelt down and quietly listened to God. I heard Him say; *"Your sins are forgiven."* I remained quiet and this time I heard, *"Enter the Threshold of my Love."* I didn't understand what **'threshold'** meant, so I asked Brother Mike, who also knew Vince, if he could explain this to me. He said that **'threshold'** was just like a wedding where one enters into a new beginning together. A **"going home"** type thing. This made a lot of sense since Vince was going to enter his new home together with God by entering the threshold of His love.

Two days before Vince died, on February 9th, he came to me in a dream to say goodbye. He told me as we embraced; **"Don't worry; I'll always be close by. I'll talk to you."** In my dream I became very emotional because I was aware of what this meant.

Then on February 11, 1995, on the Feast of Our Lady of Lourdes, Vince went home to the Mansion where God prepared a room for him, just as He had promised in a dream to his sister also a few days prior to his death. That evening while I slept I kept hearing a sentence in my head over and over again and I awoke with the same words I heard during Mass, *"BEHOLD THE THRESHOLD OF MY LOVE."* Only now the first word had changed from the original message of 'Enter' to 'Behold'. I knew without a doubt that Vince had entered the 'Threshold' of His Love. Vince had gone Home! Vince's mission on earth had ended, through his death but perhaps his mission in heaven had only just begun! My joy now lays in the knowledge that I can continue to listen with my heart not only to those I am called to assist who are dying but in the power of life that is shared even after they are physically gone.

REFLECTION: "Death of the body is but a gentle passing to a much free and fuller life. "Life Everlasting". *Francis Banks.* We are called to live from experience to experience. The shadow of death is a gruesome fact (but thank God) a fact that will never be experienced by those who listen with their hearts to hear the Truth.

Through meditation and prayer we can enter that place of silence of the soul where communion can be established with our loved ones who move on along with a connection with higher souls we call saints. We can experience a oneness with the Divine souls in heaven giving us a new perception of unity and inspiration.

What experience comes to mind that you struggled with to find meaning? Did the spirit of truth reveal itself to you? Is there someone still closely connected to you on earth and in heaven? Is there a saint that you feel closeness to, who continues to be one of your helpers? Who are the wonderful helpers who are sent to help you find meaning? How did you experience time? Does your awareness of the future become more foreseeable because of your past experiences?

Excerpts taken from Chapter 7, "A Time for Everything," in Cris Smith's Spiritual Writings, "Let the Spirit Fly Wherever It Takes You."

Chapter 13

Supernatural

*God can surprise us in how He communicates to us,
for no loving way is impossible with God*

As a small child, I found it fascinating to listen to the stories that were shared with everyone during our family story time about the nightly dramas that included the supernatural events that occurred at my parent's home town in Italy. Every relative had a ghost story to tell . . . . Needless to say, my hair would stand up on end at the very word 'devil'. Through their stories we learned so much about our culture. I realized it was their way of passing down their beliefs to us. My generation however was blessed with the opportunity of living a new life in a new country. Sometimes this caused conflict for us because we knew that, out of respect, we were to accept without question our family's ways, but we could not practice them when we were living outside our home especially if we found ourselves in school or the work force. In time I began to realize that many of the ways that were being taught to us were actually holding us back in terms of independence. In many ways I was being instilled with many fears about things that my "Canadian" friends did not share. Thankfully, because I went to College and worked part-time, I was able to experience the world outside my home. This helped me to grow and overcome many of my fears. But unfortunately, the one fear that still haunted me into my adult life was the fear of the devil.

As a teenager, I realized that the stories I grew up listening to left an impact on my soul. It seemed to me that many of the stories and practices my parents and relatives used back home in Italy to ward off evil spells touched on superstition and a delving into the occult. What was I to do? Here I was, part of a generation in this new country, that offered many job opportunities, new experiences and a chance to go to school and learn, but I had been raised in a family that carried conflicting beliefs; beliefs that they wanted so desperately to hang on to in hopes of passing them down to the next generation. I believe that during my ancestors' lives they were confronted with immoral practices where the impact of spiritism was still present. Catholics, like my ancestors, could easily and unsuspectingly have attended séances in an effort to dispel the darkness rebuking the evil spirit or "malocchio" as it is still referred to today. The problem with this is a sin of unbelief and it makes God's people believe in the symbols of Satan and less in the power of the cross. We were led to believe that pagan charms such as il corno (the love horn), or the elephants were powerful tools to ward off the evil spirits, or to protect us from curses, but what my family did not realize was that I had the greatest power of all, Jesus because He tells us to, *"Resist the devil and he will flee from you." (James 4:7)*

I loved my family and respected them but I also knew that I did not want to fall into the sin of the occult, especially because it just didn't fit into the context of being a Christian. It seemed that other young people from my generation felt the same way too. We began to ignore some of the practices that were handed down to us and started to question and search for answers. I am thankful that in my search I went looking for God who helped me in the process of listening and drew me nearer to Him.

> *"Give in to God, then; resist the devil, and he will run away from you. The nearer you go to God, the nearer God will come to you." (James 4:7-8)*

Sadly, others who broke away questioning as well, did not go in search of God but were left open to New Age spiritualism which was really not new at all. Instead, they took on a new version of warding off evil spirits like using Ouija boards, tarot cards or astrology. Teenagers today often say they are simply having fun, however, in the context of good fun the participants are opening themselves up to the occult realm. This is very dangerous because just as God will take possession of a person that opens himself up to Him in faith, so too will the devil have a claim on the person who opens himself up to him. In learning how to listen to God he helped me to overcome many fears. However, there was still that fear that seemed to overpower me and it was the fear of the evil one. I knew he was real and I could not just pretend that he wasn't around trying to scare me when I was alone, especially during the night when I couldn't sleep—but even this fear had to be overcome.

Through prayer I came to experience the supernatural in a positive and powerful way. The power of prayer can be in the form of a song or spoken out loud with words or silently with holy thoughts and sentiments. Prayers can be offered for ourselves or for the needs of others, especially the dying and the deceased. Praying to Jesus through the power of the Holy Spirit in union with all the angels and saints can also be a channel of great power for receiving what we need. The key behind this power is to "pray persistently keeping alert, giving thanks to God. (Col. 4:2) and "praying expectantly", (Psalm 5:4) believing God is listening and in our ability to listen we can hear His answer.

Prayer allows us to become powerful messengers of God on earth but, more importantly, it allows all the powers of heaven to spring into action to supply our needs. Angels, especially the ones guarding and guiding us with love and devotion, are gifts from God given to be with us, every step of our journey on earth, praying with us and helping us soar with amazing grace.

Six days before the birth of my 8th child, Sara, I lay down with my 5-year-old son named David, whom somehow ended up in bed with me. Intentionally, we both lay down at the foot of the bed so that we could capture the cool air circulating from the ceiling fan. Before retiring I read an article in one of Don Bosco's magazines. It talked about Don Boscos' nightly visits with the adversary and the torments he received from the devil that gave him no rest. Naturally this spooked me and so I decided it was time to recite my Rosary, another form of meditative prayer. Then within half an hour of falling asleep, David wakes up and sits up on the bed. I looked at him and noticed that his eyes were fixed on something or someone. "Are you okay, David?" I asked. Calmly, he responded, "Mommy, the boy's shadow just disappeared down the stair after I touched my eyes." I asked gently, "What shadow?" He pointed to the foot of the bed and said, "The shadow of the boy, who was standing right here. He was touching my hair, and when I looked to see who it was I saw the little boy. He was wearing a red shirt and pants and his hands were on his sides like this," he attempted to show me what he had seen. "But then he disappeared" he concluded somewhat disappointed. "It was cool Mommy!" were his final remarks.

I suggested to David that perhaps it might have been one of his siblings passing in the hall to go to the bathroom. "No Mommy, it was a boy." He said with such assuredness.

We ended up going back to bed and I suggested we pray "Jesus, I love you." Immediately after repeating these words, David looked up and towards the right side of the room and pointed out that his eyes were doing it again. "See Mommy, I see a man's face like Jesus smiling at me and now it disappeared."

Again there were no signs of fear on my little one's face. Eventually we ended up falling asleep. The next morning I shared everything with my husband. Don thought this was quite interesting because he also recalled experiencing a peaceful presence during the night, moments after having awakened from a dream. He remembered looking over to the night table and that the alarm clock read 2:30 a.m., unknown to him that this was the same time David had his vision.

We concluded that if the presence was peaceful and David was not afraid by it then it must be a good sign. We also thought that maybe the little boy who stood their before him, protecting and watching over him and the whole family too, might have been David's guardian angel Michael. So I prayed: Thank you Lord. Give me courage and strength from the evil one; protect us Lord. If there is meaning behind all of this and You wish me to understand it, then help me Lord, if not then I offer it all up to you. Amen.

Six Months Later: Feb. 18, 1994

I fully understood that David's guardian angel did indeed come that night to give our family hope and reassurance for events that would soon affect David. Firstly, the little boy dressed in red is a form that St. Michael did take in presenting himself to St. Catherine De Labouré. Secondly, one week after David's vision, Mary-Ann our 7th child was born and even though she was born healthy, I was left weak due to acute hemorrhaging. The following week, during my convalescing at home, David had a very serious asmatha attack for the first time ever. He was eventually hospitalized in intensive care at Sick Kids Hospital. For four days, he remained separated from the family. Due to my weakened condition and my nursing the baby, I could not be with him in his time of need. My heart ached at the thought of having David go through this without me. As tears were ready to well up within me, I suddenly felt this unexplainable reassurance and hope that everything was going to be fine. God gave me a sense of peace, and knowledge that David was safe. I understood that not only was my husband there with him but someone even greater and more powerful was with him day and night. I understood at that moment that God had sent St. Michael, as a little boy to be with David to caress him and watch over him just as he has always done. He was not alone. I thanked God for loving my child and giving us such precious gifts of our guardian angels. Prayer allowed me to focus on God and his wonderful works And teaches me to share and listen with the ears of my heart.

REFLECTION:

Through a method of visualization called imagery prayer God expects us to do his will.

Is there someone that is sick that you wish to pray for? Are you in need of prayers for healing? Then visualize yourself or the person you are praying for and see light penetrating their very being. Visualize a healthy body. In a sense every thought and expectation of what we visualize happens in the future. It is in prayer that we can create that very future. In scripture we can stand with his word and call on the power of the word to bring healing and we can call on our heavenly helpers to join us in our vision and prayers. Here are some scripture passages you can stand on for healing.

Romans 4:17 *"Call into being that which has not yet come to be."*

Isaiah 53:5 *"By his stripes I have been healed."*

Begin to confess with your mouth the love that is in your heart.

Excerpts taken from Chapter 6, "Resist the Devil", in Cris Smith's Spiritual Writings, "Let the Spirit Fly Wherever It Takes You."

Chapter 14

Miracle

Listening to God is a form of meditation. Meditation is a time to think, contemplate, reflect, ponder and consider spiritual things in God's presence. The Psalmist says: *"I meditate on your precepts and consider your ways"* (Psalm 119:15). *"I meditate on your decrees"* (Psalm 119:48). God promises us: *"Blessed is the man who does not walk in the counsel of the wicked or stand in the way of sinners or sit in the seat of mockers. But his delight is in the law of the Lord, and on His law he meditates day and night."* (Psalm 1:1-2).

While meditating on a dream I had, in which I was a child and at the same time the mother holding myself as a child, I came to understand that the child symbolized that I was a child of God and just as a mother would hold her child to protect them, I too was to hold onto my faith and protect it.

During this period of my life, I discovered solace in going into my room and spending time with the Lord through imagery prayer. This form of prayer allowed me to use my imagination to enter into meditation. The Rosary in many ways helped me do this too. While all the mysteries of the Rosary helped me experience the life of Jesus nothing seemed to touch me more than the sorrowful mysteries. It seemed that the passion of our Lord united me the most with Jesus. I imagined myself in the Garden of Gethsemane with Jesus while He prayed at the rock. With my eyes closed and in a moment of quiet and peace I found myself connecting and listening to Jesus.

Years earlier, I unknowingly experienced a powerful manifestation through imagery prayer, when I first read about our Blessed Mother. I meditated on her life on earth, her role in our lives, all through a book entitled; "Meditations of Mary" and I discovered that I was becoming emotionally attached to her and the sacrifices she endured especially as she stood watching her Son die. I felt as if I was truly there with her. I could see in my mind Joseph of Arimathaea taking Jesus' body off the cross and layng His lifeless body on His mother's lap. I could hear Mary, Our Blessed Mother, crying during this heart-wrenching moment that she was forced to endure. My heart sobbed with hers and tears flowed down my face as I experienced the same sorrow that was piercing her heart. I finally understood the prophecy that was spoken by Simeon to Our Lady, on the day Jesus was brought to the temple for the presentation, **'and a sword will pierce your heart!"** For years, every time I saw a Michaelangelo's famous statue, Pietà of Our Lady holding the lifeless body of Jesus on her lap, the sorrowful emotions would well up within me.

But never were these emotions as profound, as when my, little baby Sara died. Every day after her funeral, I prayed that God would allow me to have a spiritual connection with Sara. I lamented to my poor husband in those moments of weakness how much I wanted to hear from God and to receive a sign. The Lord answered my prayers.

It happened one evening after telling my husband, how much I wanted a spiritual connection with Sara. He suggested we all pray the Rosary together before putting the little ones to bed. I agreed because I wanted to continue praying with my whole family, as we did when Sara was alive. Ten minutes into our prayer which happened to be the Rosary, I fell asleep. As I sat on the edge of the kid's beds, Don left me there hoping that I would get some rest. This is when I received my vision.

I saw myself downstairs in my living room holding Sara in my arms and walking around with her as I had done numerous times when she was alive. As I held her directly in front of me, I noticed how precious and beautiful she was. She no longer carried the facial deformities and I noticed how alert she was as she stared straight at me. Then I paused for a moment to stare back at her as she gently lifted her right hand and with her tiny thumb blessed me on my forehead three times, each time making the sign of the cross. I yelled for Don in my dream to come quickly so he too could see Sara and as he stood next to me we smiled at each other. Then he nodded and patted my head, as if to say, "I knew you'd get your sign." Then I awoke refreshed and at peace.

The second sign happened three weeks into my bereavement. It was a Saturday evening and I decided to go to Mass. It was a special Mass that included grade two students receiving their First Holy Communion. Just looking at the beautiful little girls was enough to make me cry, especially the last little girl at the end of the procession who walked up carrying a crown of roses to present to the statue of Mary. As I stared at her I thought of Sara and I prayed to Mother Mary and asked her to watch over my Sara, even though in my heart I knew she was.

Since Sara's death, I found myself always crying during the consecration and especially after receiving the Eucharist. My spiritual director explained to me that this was happening because Sara was most present, during the communion of saints.

That same evening as I was putting my little ones to sleep, I began to cry again. I tried to explain to my husband that I just wanted another sign. Don made me understand that I wasn't really giving anyone up there a chance to talk to me because I wasn't listening. That night Don prayed over me and asked that I find a way to listen and connect with Sara. Not being able to sleep that evening, I decided to go downstairs and make myself a cup of tea. As I took the last sip of my tea, I looked down into the bottom of my cup and saw my own reflection and immediately I heard; ***"Look into the mirror and see me for I am a part of you. A part of your reflection."*** Then as I returned to bed feeling somewhat consoled, I closed my eyes and a tune began to play in my head with the words from a song that I played to Sara when she was alive. Over and over again, I heard,

"In your loving arms we lay this wondrous gift."

Then I heard this angelic voice sing those same words in a soft and soothing voice. Then she spoke directly to me and asked me.

"Isn't it a wondrous gift?"

"Yes." I answered.

She continued to ask, **"Didn't you get to hold this wondrous gift?"**

"Yes." I repeated fervently.

"Then", she firmly yet gently proceeded to explain;

"Let this gift live on in you, snap out of it before it begins to do damage to you."

"Okay." I responded.

Difficult as it was to open my eyes, I finally did, only to notice that the time was 3:00a.m. (The Hour of Mercy).

I knew somehow that this voice I heard belonged to Mother Mary, who had come to answer my prayer. Not only was she watching out for Sara as I had asked of her but I knew that she had been taking care of me too.

In the midst of all my sorrow God was allowing me to experience His joy. One month after we buried Sara I began writing in my journal again entitling it, **"My New Journey With The Lord'**, in this way I could never doubt how much I was loved by God. With a renewed sense of confidence I could "Go and lie down" as did Samuel when he followed the directions of Eli the prophet, in the bible. I too could say like Samuel, "Speak Lord for your servant is listened"

We can individually find that right time/moment to meditate, pray or contemplate and discover which method best speaks to our hearts. One form of prayer that I have found to be effective is imagery prayer. It is a form of contemplative prayer or as St. Ignatius calls it "spiritual exercises." The goal is to draw a person into a real, living, growing relationship with Jesus. The exercise embraces an understanding of both the heart and the mind. It is not a prayer of words but of imagination that allows you to enter into the image you are wanting to experience. It is also a way of spending time with God every day. Let me share with you some of the preparation for this form of prayer. First find a quiet place where you will not be disturbed or distracted. Take a comfortable, relaxed position. Close your eyes and focus on your breathing. Inhale and exhale deep, long breaths. Then with your imagination pick a place where you can go that allows you to feel God's loving presence. For me many times I go to a room which is filled with light. There are times I see myself on a sandy beach and the sun is shining down on me. There are times when I go to places I have read in the bible especially places where I know that Jesus is. The Garden of Gethsemane is one such place where I know that Jesus is praying at the rock. I quietly imagine myself approaching Jesus and quietly sit next to him. Comfort and peace fill my heart as I begin to feel the Lord's presence. I see a light surrounding me, warming my whole being. I invite you to try this as you allow yourself to experience the positive emotions that come with this spiritual exercise. If any negative emotions from the past surface allow His light to enter your mind, and help you to transform these memories into happy memories that you will attempt to recall yourself. If happy memories surface relive them place yourself back into that memory and experience all the positive emotions. If you experience pain anywhere in your body, let His light enter this area and see the healing that you are hoping for. You can read another personal experience in regards to this in chapter 16. Another form of prayer that has helped me is music. Music helps me to quiet my soul and focus my mind and heart. Playing music throughout my day helps me to reflect on my time of prayer. The more we spend time to walk with Jesus the more he will reveal himself to you. The greatest thing we will hear in our hearts when we listen is his love.

REFLECTION: No thought, desire or fear is as strong as a vision that comes from God. When we pray in the correct fashion we are not asking God to do something. God is inspiring us to act in his place. The point of all being is love and everything you love is what makes life worth living. Love requires a listening heart that is alive, awake and free. List all things you LOVE. I love my role as _____, I love being _____ I love eating_____ I love my child or children _____, I love books _____, I love watching _____ etc . . . Fill in the blanks

Don't edit yourself; don't worry about prioritizing or anything of that sort. Whether it's the people in your life or the things that bring you joy or the places that are dear to you, you could not love them if you didn't have a loving heart.

Excerpts taken from Chapter 9, "Sharing the Passion of Christ", from Cris Smith's Spiritual Writings, "Let the Spirit Fly Wherever It Takes You."

Chapter 15

Held in the Palm of His Hand

God's kindness gave me the opportunity to accomplish what He had already planned for me long ago.

While sitting in the waiting room of my doctor's office one day in October, four months after the death of our baby Sara, I found myself talking to a middle-aged woman who began to share with me her physical and emotional problems. I was so moved by this woman's sadness that I wanted to give her my miraculous medal (kissed by Mother Teresa) for comfort. I had received it as a gift from Martez, a nun from Mother Teresa's order. However, since I did not act on this initial inspiration right away, by the time I decided to do so, she was gone.

Early that morning I had prayed, "God, how can I unite with You this pain of grief I still carry in my heart on the loss of my child?" Was this his way of answering me?

Days later I returned to the doctor's office for my follow-up appointment and as I sat down waiting to be called, I quietly prayed my Chaplet of Divine Mercy. This is a prayer that was taught by Sister Faustina after she had a vision of Jesus who revealed the words to her. Eventually two women came out into the waiting room from the doctor's office and sat down next to me. I sensed anguish on the young face of one of the women. Then the doctor ushered me into his office and he apologetically explained that he was dealing with a patient who needed immediate help. During my visit with the doctor, his receptionist knocked on the door and interrupted our visit. He excused himself, telling me that he needed to take an urgent phone call from another doctor. I quickly determined that the young woman he was so concerned about must have been the one that sat next to me in the waiting room. When the doctor returned he confirmed my suspicions and told me that he had a patient who was suicidal.

He ushered me off with a clean bill of health but not before I was able to tell him that I would pray for that woman. As I was prepared to leave, something inside of me told me that I needed to do more than just pray so with holy boldness, I knocked on the door of the examining room where I knew the doctor was in with the woman. The doctor opened the door and stared at me surprised to see me standing there. I think he thought I had forgotten something because he moved forward in an attempt to shield the patient and shut the door behind him. I quickly asked him if I could give my miraculous medal that I held in my hand to that young woman in his office. Perplexed by my request, the kind doctor noticed that the woman was paying attention and so he gently moved back and allowed me to act on my inspiration. Thankfully I moved towards her and said:

> *"I just wanted to give you this medal that was kissed by Mother Teresa."*

With a sad look she came towards me and stretched her hand out in acceptance. I placed the medal into the palm of her hand and told her that I felt compelled to give it to her. Without saying a word, she closed her fist around the medal and raised it close to her heart. She accepted my gift and with tears flowing down her face, she looked directly into my eyes. Somehow we understood each others pain. I told her that the medal was given to me and was very special. As I placed my hand upon her arm, I felt compelled to tell her that I lost a baby in May. As tears flowed down my cheeks I explained that I was okay now because I knew my baby was in heaven. God was taking care of me and helping me heal, so I told her that I wanted her to have this medal and that she would be okay too.

Then with the power of the Holy Spirit I assured her that she was loved. I repeated these words again slower and with great confidence. ***"You are loved!"***

Her face and eyes lit up with a look of joyous expectancy. I could see the heavy burden she carried momentarily lifted. I hugged her and said, "God bless you." With tears streaming down my face, I said goodbye and left.

I continued to pray for this young woman and asked Mother Teresa to intercede my requests to God. For weeks I prayed that the young woman would be healed of her temptations and seek the graces of God. I had no doubt that this young woman's life would be different if she allowed herself to be open to God's word and touch. This experience left me with an overwhelming feeling of joy because, *I knew that . . . "all things work together for good to those who love God" (Romans 8:28)*

Two weeks later a good friend visited the same doctor. Without any prior knowledge of the events of my personal visit, she happened to mention my name in a general conversation. According to my friend, the doctor, upon hearing my name, could not hold back his excitement as he personally shared with her what he called in his own words a "miracle". He gave her an account of what transpired with the young woman, without breaching any confidence, and then added that he was prepared to write to the medical association outlining the details of this young woman's miraculous progress. He truly believed that the progress in her emotional state occurred as a result of her receiving the miraculous medal. He said, "Cris gave her something to believe in." My friend was touched by all that he said and felt compelled to share it with me.

> *"O Lord, I will honor and praise your name for you are my God; you do such wonderful things! (Isaiah 25:1)*

The story doesn't end here. Martez heard about this story and felt compelled to share something with me. She believed this would help me better understand the wonderful things God does for us. She began her story by telling me that on the day of Mother Teresa's death, a distressed couple came to Mother Teresa, the sisters suggested that they come back and see her another day but Mother Teresa asked them to let the couple in. The couple were parents who had just recently lost their teenage child to suicide. Mother Teresa was saddened in not being able to help this child sooner. All she could do was pray for them. She later shared with her Sisters that she felt the pain this couple carried in their hearts. Sister Martez wanted me to know that God in His mercy allowed me; a mother who also carried the same pain of grief like this couple was blessing me and using me as His instrument to help save the teenage soul I met in the doctor's office, before it was too late. The miraculous medal I gave away that was kissed by

Mother Teresa was God's way of using his faithful servant, Mother Teresa, to continue her work on earth by interceding for this young woman also.

Days after this experience happened in the doctor's office, I was taken totally by surprise by a letter I received from a woman named Trish who had an inoperable brain tumor and whom I promised to pray for almost five years ago. Well, how can I not see this as God's way of speaking to me through the pain in my heart. What joy to know that he speaks to all of us and together we can heal and experience His Joy!

Trish's letter:

Dear Cris:

It has been a long time since we have talked. I think of you often and I hope this letter finds you and yours well. I was clearing through some papers and found your original letter to me, dated Feb. 26, 1997. What a road we have traveled since then. I can hardly believe it is coming up to five years since I was originally diagnosed with a brain tumor. Your love and support was so greatly appreciated when I truly needed a friend. I will never be able to thank you enough for all that you have given me. The last time we spoke was shortly after you lost your baby daughter Sara. I still read the story you wrote about her in the "Salesian", it gives me courage, strength and compassion when things sometimes become difficult. As Thanksgiving draws near and I think of the many things I have to be thankful for, I wanted to include you in that list. Life is good. I am healthy, my family is all well and healthy, and I am truly grateful to the good Lord for the gifts he has given me. The times of trouble that have fallen on many in the US and other countries who have lost their loved ones has encouraged me to be more appreciative for the many blessings that have been bestowed upon me.

You are in my thoughts and prayers. Keep well and God bless. Trish.

REFLECTION: *That same day I went to reflect on words I read in a book called "He and I" a book of inspirational words shared by Jesus to a mystic, I came across a passage that made me realize how much God was speaking to me.*

It seemed like these words penned so long ago were written for me to read at this moment in time so that its message could speak to my heart. I invite you to read, reflect and allow the words to speak to your heart.

"It is always now. Didn't you understand that when you were in Jerusalem and prayed on Calvary? Tenderly offer your sacrifice for the world. Aren't there others weaker than you? Can they rise up without me? If you wanted to save a person very dear to you and this beloved person refused your help, how much you would suffer! I want to help the world, and the world refuses My help. Speak to the Father about His Son on the cross, so that he will let Himself be touched and send light to these hardened ones who do not even look at Me, You know how one speaks to a father who is watching his son die? Won't this father hasten to carry out his child's last wishes? Remind Him of the words, 'Forgive them for they know not what they do." It is always now. And if He forgives, what will He not do.

Do you know the outpouring of any love like His? A love that is all readiness. It is now this love. It is always now."

Excerpts taken from Chapter 9, Sharing the Passion of Christ, from Cris Smith's Spiritual writings in "Let the Spirit Fly Wherever It Takes You"

Chapter 16

Reliving Happy Moments

The most recent experience that touched me in a profound and personal way happened while I was visiting my dad who still lives in the home I grew up in. While searching in the attic for an old story book, in one of the dresser drawers I found something else totally unexpected. It was an envelope that belonged to my mom and in it were prayer cards dating back to 1991 which seemingly she used to pray with. Since dad had donated most of her things a year after her death it was a joyful surprise to come across something, anything that had belonged to her. Needless to say I stopped searching for the book, and was now drawn to reflect on another story that seemed to unfold before my very eyes.

In the envelope were prayer cards with pictures of various saints on the front side of the card and a prayer on the back. Some cards were in English and some in Italian. Then as I continued to flip through the prayer cards, I noticed two pictures that had been placed in the centre of one of the prayer cards; one picture was of me taken when I was seven years old and the other one of Gino, my godchild. Gino is my sister Mary's twenty year old son, who must have been no more than three years old at the time the picture was taken. I was touched at the thought that my mom would have these pictures tucked away in her prayer cards. The thought that she might have been praying for me or my nephew was moving to say the least but more importantly it was the confirmation I received that the Lord was speaking to me through this memorable discovery.

The day before, during my quiet prayer time, I came across a spiritual exercise in which I was asked to reflect on a happy childhood memory. By allowing my imagination to reflect on my life story and recalling this past happy childhood memory, I could once again relive the same emotions of joy and happiness in the present moment. The meditation was a teaching on how to work through our negative emotions from the past so that we can experience the impact of the positive emotions when we reflect on happy memories. By making it a point to relive these happy memories, our mind relives all the positive emotions that are associated with them and in turn this creates a positive impact on our health and rejuvenates us.

 I attempted to do this meditation and went back into my childhood memories as far as I could recall—at least fifty years back. I was a little frustrated at first that I could not think of any memories that occurred during my fourth or fifth year of life but then I thought of one that occurred when I was seven years old. The one positive memory that I had unknowingly imprinted in my memory, was the very same vision that was recorded in that 3x5 photograph my mother had safely tucked away in her prayer cards. It was un-canning how my reflection exercise the day before had revealed to me the same memory that was captured in that photo, forty eight years ago. This memory moved me as I saw myself wearing the same dress in my vision and it triggered more memories as I saw the white shoes I wore with it. Then the memory became alive as I saw myself dancing with my Uncle Joe who taught me how to ballroom dance to the tango, waltz and cha cha cha. Looking at the picture I saw the happy child in me, and once again I could feel the free spirit that lived in my soul, easily willing to fly wherever it took me. This was a wonderful chapter of my life which included childhood memories of my cousins and the time we spent together visiting them during our summer vacation. I distinctly remember the Beetle Volkswagen my Uncle Domenic owned and all the adventures we took joy riding together with my cousins in his car as we all sat on top of each other laughing and sticking our heads out of the window. All these childhood adventures filled my heart and I was now reliving it all with a happy smile on my face. How ironic it was that this picture was taken on August 1963 and today I stood holding it in my hand forty eight years later, on August 2011. Transcending time and space, the past became my present, if just for a moment as I sat on the bed in the attic holding this picture. The Lord manifested my joyful childhood experiences and spoke to me through my mom's prayers. He revealed not only the blessings he poured onto me and my family but how He used—my mom—and her beautiful character—as His instrument to invoke the aid of all the saints to pray for us.

This day was not over yet, as this experience continued to touch a few other people in my family. In particular my sister Mary whom I immediately called to share with her what had just transpired in the attic and to reveal to her that the other picture my mom had in the prayer cards was that of her twenty year old son Gino. Mary immediately felt that this was also a sign of confirmation for her. She experienced the Lord's peace knowing that He had heard her prayer which she had prayed moments before I called her and in which she had also invoked the aid of our earthly mother to watch over her son Gino. My sister's motherly concern for her own son Gino weighted heavy on her heart since he was away in Italy on a University course and had not spoken to him for a few days. Her desire for a sign that Gino was safe came as the Lord spoke his peace to her and revealed that our mom had been praying for him for years.

We both felt that this was without a doubt the Lord's way of speaking to our hearts, reassuring us that our mother's prayers were heard and that she continues to look out for us in heaven.

Amazing how a simple 'sign' like all the signs I experienced on this day helped me to see the Lord's presence in everything and hear his powerful message of love above all joy and peace. What seemed hidden, lost and forgotten was brought to light, illuminating and displaying truth.

This day felt like I had given birth to a new life once again. To find an object or to have a recollection of a memory that brings back positive emotions is such a beautiful message of love that brings us closer to the Lord and with our loved ones. Once I realized that the picture my mom had tucked away in her prayer cards was of me, this feeling magnified even more. Just knowing that I shared a special spot in her prayer life amongst all the saints she so venerated, was something I felt grateful for. The Lord spoke to me through a memorabilia revealing truth and love. A simple object left behind provided one more opportunity for the Lord to draw me near to him . . . even 15 years after my mom's death, enkindling my soul and reigniting my heart full of paternal love from my Heavenly Father.

REFLECTION: Facts verses stories. Jesus spoke in stories why? Because facts speak to the mind but stories speak to the heart. The best stories are the ones that bring us eternal truth. They remind us that things are not always what they seem. We live in 2 worlds or better still we live in one world with 2 parts. In one world we see and the other we cannot see. We have a crucial role to play in our story of life but we doubt our role. We see it as mundane when in fact we are very special. It is hard to believe but when we get a glimpse through happy memories that can open the eyes of our heart it will change everything. Love is the life of the heart says St. Francis de Sales. St. Paul tells us to not lose heart and to look at life with the eyes of our heart. Eph 1:18.

When we see and hear with the eyes and ears of our heart, we discover an awakening.

Ask yourself—Is there some glimpse you can recall as you relive your happy memories that reveal your true self and could there really be some hidden greatness in you?

Are you spending time to recall some happy memories in silence and solitude?

What does your heart need? Start by asking God what do you have for my heart?

Jesus always asked what do you want? He took them back into his desire. Why? It is where we must go if we are to meet God. He is continually taking them into their hearts. What we need is life. The heart is life so we look at our heart and it reveals our life story. Where are you in the story of life?

How will your next chapter unfold?

Look at your connections. Who are you being called to live in fellowship of the heart?

Is it family, community or both?

Chapter 17

Stirring in my Heart

*Something we sense with a solid sense of peace and love around it.
This stirring often is God speaking to our souls.*

On January 27th, 2009, I picked up my 10-year-old daughter, Stephanie from school who wasn't feeling well. On the way home I told Stephanie I needed to pop into the Salvation Army store. The store was just up the road from where we lived, and I wanted to see if I could find inexpensive items to use them as props in our youth programs. I suppose it really could have waited since Stephanie wasn't feeling well, but for some reason I just felt compelled to go into the store at that particular moment. Perhaps you know what I mean—it's one of those moments when you feel the need to do or say something. If you act on it, you will find you will experience a peace beyond understanding. Without a doubt this was one of those moments for me.

Inside the store, while waiting for me, Stephanie searched through the used book section hoping to find a book that might interest her. As I made my way over to Stephanie to help her look for one, I happened to come across a hard covered book that caught my eye and at a second glance I noticed that it was an "Inspirational Journal". Stephanie saw my interest and when I told her this was a blank journal, she immediately knew I would claim it as my own, because I LOVE journals! Being an avid journal writer, I always find it exciting when I come across unique, colorful and best of all affordable journals that I can use to record my thoughts, dreams, stories, reflections, teachings, inspirations, etc.

Now, this particular journal, I held in my hands attracted me for a few reasons. First of all, the book was a hard cover, and had beautiful scenery of the ocean, splashing waves, rocks, and a lighthouse painted in a natural and symbolic way. As I flipped through the blank pages I noticed each page of the journal had 6 reflective questions to engage the writer to reflect on. Printed on these pages where the following questions,

1. What did I do today for the one I love?
2. What did I do today for the ones I love?
3. What was my favorite moment or event today?
4. What did I do today towards the realization of my goals?
5. What new ideas, thoughts, and discoveries did I make today?
6. Other reflections, emotions, or events I experienced today?

I saw these questions being used as a way of inviting the writing to reflect on things that deal with both the heart and soul and this enticed me even more to own this journal. So, I continued to flip through the pages in the journal until I landed on a page that immediately revealed something more about itself. This was NOT just an old blank journal that had simply appeared from nowhere, instead this journal had in fact a starting point with a date, Gennaio-1-2005, along with a name and address of the one that it had been entrusted to.

My first reaction was that perhaps this journal was not one that I could use since it had already belonged to another person but I couldn't bring myself to putting it down just yet. Instead I continued to flip through the next few pages trying to convince myself that this journal was a special find. I told myself I could always erase the few pages that had been used by simply tearing them out. In this way I would be protecting the previous owners' privacy before using it as my own journal to record my own personal thoughts and emotions—especially the ones that deal with the Lord and me. However, my mind and my spirit were not in sync. My mind was telling me that it didn't make any sense to purchase a used journal that belonged to someone else, but my soul was telling me that there was something special about this journal and I felt a certain connection to it. So as I kept flipping the pages of the journal, I discovered that there were only three entries made in the entire book and what caught my eye was the date of the first entry—January 27, 2005 Wow! Was this just a coincidence, or should I say *God incidence* that I was holding this journal in my hands on the very same date, January 27th, only four years later. Well, that was all I needed to read at that moment to know that the book was coming home with me. I decided that the journal was worth buying. Even though I only paid 99 cents for it, I knew that it was worth much more and it was something I would treasure.

This journal, no doubt found its way to me so I took it home and I placed it on my kitchen table. A few days later on January 31st it ended up in my bedroom on my nightstand. That same night after getting home from a family birthday party, I went to bed, but couldn't fall asleep. It was 2:00 am in the morning and I decided to write in my journal when I noticed that the new-found journal was laying on my nightstand. Maybe due to my curiosity or because the Lord planned it this way, I felt I needed to find out why I felt drawn to this person's journal.

In the quiet and stillness of this particular moment my curiosity got the better of me and I began to read what was written.

The first question answered in the journal was:

Question #1: What did I do today for the one I love?

She writes:

27 Gennaio, 2005

> *"Oggi era il mio speciale giorno 50 annie sposato sono stata triste che nessuno si sono ricordato a spettato tutto il giorno ela sera nessuno mia chiamato pero domenica dopo mezzo giorno sono uscito e sono andata a comprare la pizza la metta melo mangiato fuore che il sole seduto e poi mio mangiato unaltra alla cucina e odetto Giuseppe oggi ci siamo sposata dopo mezo giorno di Domenica 50 fa e tutto epassato ma ringrazio a mia suora mia chiamata un giorno prima ma se ricordata grazie di nuovo io lo so che mi pensa perche mi chiama spesso. Grazie di nuovo Maria che Dio ti benedice sempre anch quando non ci sono. Livia*

English Translation:

January 27, 2005

Today was my special day 50 years married. I am sad because no one has remembered. I waited all day and night but no one called me. But Sunday afternoon I went out to buy pizza. Half of it I ate outside as I sat alone and then I ate another piece in the kitchen. I said Guiseppe today we were married in the afternoon on a Sunday 50 years ago. It has all passed away but I thank my sister who called me the day before. At least she remembered. Thank you again I know that she thinks of me because she calls me often. Thank you again Maria and may God bless you always even when I am no longer here. Livia

I noticed that her handwriting was legible and written in Italian with a European calligraphy that reminded me so much of my own mother's handwriting. The first few lines gave me the impression that she was sad and immediately drew me into her life. On her first entry, she recorded the date at the top of the page, to acknowledge her special day—her 50th wedding anniversary. Unbelievably, this woman's entry reminded me of my parents and their anniversary which happens to be on January 28th—the very next day.

She shares the reason for her sadness in the next line. She accepts the reality that no one has remembered this special day and this tugs at my heartstrings as I continue to read. She speaks to the spirit of her late husband Giuseppe, as if he were still present and with her in the kitchen. With just these few words, I can feel her heart saddened by the loss of her husband and I sense the grief of this elderly widow, who now finds herself alone and undoubtedly waits for her own destiny to unfold.

The last line of her first entry reveals to me her gentle resignation to her lot in life, her gratefulness and faith. She wishes her sister blessings as she records the fact that her sister Maria is the only one who remembered her anniversary—even though she called a day early. Once again, I am drawn to this Italian mother figure, which helps me to see that I too missed my own parents' anniversary, which was on January 28th. Through this woman, I was able to spend time with God and reflect on my own negligence of not having called my Dad to share in his special memories of having been married to my mom for what would have been 53 years, had my mother still been alive.

The second entry is dated 1 Febraio. (I was reading this entry at 2:00 a.m. in the morning on Feb. 1st)

Here again I could not help but think of this un-canning moment where the dates are coinciding.

Question 2: What did I do today for the ones I love?

She writes:

1 Febraio

> *"il mio nome e Livia dunque oggi sono uscita affare le massaggi ma dopo che siamo mangiato nel sisturin dove vado guardavamo la televisione e la staff mi chiama separata dove mia detto che aveva morta mia nibe vicino mia dispiaciuto molto ma chesi puo fare e che il Signore la da il riposo. Livia*

English Translation:

February 1st

> *My name is Livia. Well today I went out to get a massage. But after I went to eat in the ???? where we go to watch television and the staff calls me separately where she tells me that my roommate (or neighbor I am not sure) died. I am very saddened by this but what can we do. May God give her rest. Livia*

Third entry dated 2 Febraio

Question #3: What did I do today for the ones I love?

She writes:

2 Febraio

"*sono ricevuto una grande sopresa che Toni e Maria mie venuto a visitare abbiamo parlato per me ariguardo che si prendera la mia responsabilita per me ali domani puo succedere qual cosa. Mia detto di si che loro prendera la risponsabilita per me se succide qual cosa io aviso al loficio qui e gli do il telefono di Toni e Maria e di Anna Maria.*"

English Translation:

February 2nd

"*I received a great surprise. Toni and Maria came to visit me and we talked about them being my guardian and taking my responsibilities in the event that one day something might happen to me. They told me yes that they would take the responsibility of me in the event that something happens to me. I will advise the office and I will give them the telephone number of Toni and Maria and of Anna Maria.*"

By the second and third entries, I felt I was being given a deeper understanding of how much we are all connected by God's Spirit of unity and I noticed that her last entry was written with joy, a joy that only God could have given her in the midst of all her sorrow.

Question #4: What was my favorite moment or event today?

She writes:

Sono stato al longe (I think she means lounge) con gli amici e doppe molto.

English Translation:

> *I was in the longe (*I think she means lounge*) with my friends after a long time*

> **Question #5: What did I do today towards the realization of my goals?**

She writes:

> "*today sono pintato un quaderno e valentina carta con i fiori per me e questo sara un ricordo e sulla mia eta.*

English Translation:

> "*today I painted a workbook and a valentine card with flowers for me and this will be a rememberence of my age.*

> **Question #6: What new ideas, thoughts, discoveries did I make today?**

She writes:

> *o discovere tuday che estato una buona giornata sono uscita e sono andata al lona con i miei amici sono fatta un po di spesa e omangiato cinese fund ela meta melo portato a casa ringrazio ancora Dio*

English Translation:

> *I discoverd today that I had a good day. I went out and I wend at Iona with my firneds. I did a little bit of grocery shopping and I ate Chinese Food. Half of it I brought back home. I thank God once again*

She then pens what might have been her last entry on earth with such a beautiful closing prayer in which she asks God to bless and protect her family, friends and finally herself.

2 Febraio, 2005

"*mi sento bene grazia a Dio e sono le 2 della notte e ora con lamice preghiera che la mia famiglia dorme ed io preghero per loro e Dio gli da un buon riposo a tutti. Grazia ancora mio Gesu che io ti amo e tu mi proteggi a giorno e notte.*

Livia

February 2, 2005

I feel good thank God and it is 2:00 a.m. in the morning and now in union with my prayer warriors I pray that my family sleeps and I pray for them that God will give them all a good rest. Thank you again my Jesus. I love you and may you protect me day and night.

Livia

After reading these last entries, I felt I needed to pray for this woman. It was 3:00 a.m. in the morning, so I prayed the Divine Mercy prayer. As I stared at the journal, I knew then and there that this journal did not fall into my hands by chance, but rather it came to me as an invitation for me to continue writing in her journal. Therefore, I knew the pages were not to be erased or torn out, but cherished and shared. I believe Livia was used as a witness and testimony of God's timeless love and that God used her as an example to show us all how He can transcend time and use each and everyone one of us to become extra ordinary.

I read the entries over again many times and trying to piece together what her life might have been like. Based on what Livia writes in her second entry, it seems she lived in a nursing home and I imagined she may have moved or passed away shortly after recording her last entry and that perhaps the staff or family member who donated her belongings did not realize there were entries in her journal. Also, since one of her entries talks about Toni and Maria who came to visit her and who also agreed to be her guardians in case something happened to her suggests she did not have any children or that she was not closely connected to them. I envisioned her in her mid 70's and I concluded that her name Livia might be short for Olivia.

Reading her personal experience and understanding how she may have felt alone and disappointed, reminded me of my duties as a daughter to my own elderly father who, like Livia, is also a widow and lives alone. More importantly, I realized the need for me to put my love into action. Days later when I finally called my dad, I shared with him this adventure of my journal discovery. He in turn, shared with me his experience on, January 28th, his anniversary day, when he felt my mom's spiritual presence very close to him all day long. He also said that he bought roses in honour of their anniversary and brought them to her when he visited her grave.

ADDITIONAL ENTRY MADE TWO YEARS LATER

A few months after this JOURNAL ADVENTURE, I went to the address that was recorded in the Journal, in hopes of possibly meeting Livia or at least figuring out where she had gone. With my husband and my children at my side, we drove to the address, and soon realized that it was an Ontario housing complex. My two daughters and I found the courage to go up to the 5th floor (this too was providence as a woman allowed us in through the front door). We knocked a few times but there was no answer. We tried one last time and this time the neighbor across the hall opened her door and asked if she could help us. I inquired about Livia and she informed me that Livia moved away a few months earlier. Her daughter helped her move but she wasn't sure where she had gone to live. It was a relief to know that Livia was still alive and that she had a daughter. However not knowing all the details of her life I wondered if she was healthy and happy. To this day, I continue to think of her and pray for her. One day I know that we will meet in that spiritual realm where all souls go. Once again, we will connect with everyone who has crossed our path on earth, both physically and spiritually. We can only hope that we have done what is right and just on earth. I pray that our peace and eternal happiness will be complete when it is time for all of us to meet again and I end this chapter with a prayer and reflection.

Let us pray:

Lord thank you for allowing us to experience the communion of saints. We are all connected in the Body of Christ. May we all continue to witness to each other this grace of life and death. We give you thanks for all the graces you bestow on us as we continue to grow in Spirit loving unconditionally. May you always be praised and glorified. In Jesus' name we pray. Amen.

Chapter 18

Secret Code of Love

Occasionally through the charismatic gifts of knowledge, prophecy, healing and tongues we find that God unites in our thoughts a sense of truth because it accompanies peace and love.

Greta was an incredible woman from my church community who had immigrated to Canada from her hometown of Ireland many years ago. At a young age, Greta was left a widow to care for her five children alone. Witnessing her sense of peace and strength I decided one day to ask her how she could survive this loss of a spouse, coupled with the challenges of raising five children alone in a new country and still find the strength to carry on with such a giving and loving spirit. She recognized my fear in this question and calmly explained, *"God's grace comes when we need it and not before"* and then proceeded to explain further with an example of a true story about Corrie Ten Boom, a survivor of the Holocaust. She said, "When Corrie, the author, was a young girl, her father helped her understand the meaning of grace by using the example of a train conductor who went around collecting the money for the cost of the tickets on the train. He asked her, *"When do I give you the money for the train ticket?"* Her reply was, *"When we see the ticket master coming towards us."* He assured her that this is when God gives us the grace, when we are coming towards our moment of need."

Her words were prophetic because in my greatest need, which was the death of my baby, God not only gave me the grace I needed, but with it He gave me a deep understanding of what grace is. To be open to God's graces means to be open to life. Being open to life is what has enabled my husband and I to grow stronger in the virtues of faith, hope and love. This much we understood.

The birth of every one of our children made us aware of how much God is present in our lives. We are in awe at His wonderful work of art. We know that each child is a gift from God that He has allowed us to be a part of, in order that they may fulfill His purpose. As a married couple, Don and I are honoured to be allowed to co-create with the Father, and be a part of this miracle of life.

> **"God is love . . . Perfect love casts out fear. We love because he first loved us." (1 John 4:18)**

These words impacted my life twenty five years ago when I began to practice my faith again but the day Sara was born, these words took on a profound new meaning.

Twenty-five years ago, I invented a secret code for the words I LOVE YOU so that my husband and I could use it whenever we were in situations that made it difficult for us to say it openly in public. Our secret code was the number 122. The number 122 represented the sum total of the equivalent numerical value for each of the letters in the words I love you. For years, we have amusingly used this code in greeting cards, birthday cakes, and any other special occasions that came up in our lives together. Sara's birth was one of those special occasions. Her birth left its mark on both our hearts. It allowed us to come to know God in a direct and personal way.

You see, after the doctors had finished doing a preliminary assessment of Sara's condition, he informed us that her problems were very serious. After attending to Sara's immediate needs as well as mine, the nurses gave me time to be alone. Suddenly I became scared. I could no longer hold back my tears and I started to cry. I asked God to give me strength and to be with me. I pleaded with Him to not leave me and asked in desperation, **"Oh, God, Where are you?"** In complete submission, I continued to pray in this manner until a nurse quietly entered my room and I suddenly felt compelled to know what time the baby was born. So I asked her, **"At what time was the baby born?"** It was as if everything that had just transpired depended on my knowing her time of birth, the time that she made her entry into this world. As if, somehow, knowing this piece of information would make a difference. The nurse told me in a compassionate voice. **"Sara was born at 1:22 a.m."**

God had suddenly hugged my heart! At that moment I knew, without a doubt, that God had answered my prayer. In my heart I heard him saying, "*I am with you, my child, I always have been.* **I LOVE YOU!**" said my **ABBA!** "**I am a part of your secret code of love which is the manifestation of my love. Be not afraid, my child, I go before you. Come, follow me, and I will give you rest. I have sent you my messengers helping you prepare the way. Never alone."**

The number 122 was God's message of love speaking directly to our hearts. By listening with the ears of our heart we understood that we were being invited to trust and follow Him.

This miracle also gave my husband the strength and courage to go on. **"That's all I need to know"** he said. We both understood something of His love for us. We both knew that Sara was conceived as the incarnation of our love with God. I also sensed that God was saying, **"See, I have carved her on the palm of my hand and there she still lays. See what I have given you through this precious gift of life. I have placed my signature on this wondrous work of art and signed it with the Number 122!**

> "God is love . . . Perfect love casts out all fear." We love because he first loved us." (1 John 4:18)

With gratitude, my husband and I continued to live our lives open to God's graces, by being open to the greatest grace of all—the grace of LIFE! This is what grace is: God's gift of his divine love and life for us all, especially through the presence of the Holy Spirit in our hearts. With the help of the Holy Spirit we can carry out the most difficult task. St. Paul says:

> **"I can do all things through Him who strengthens me.**
> **(Phil 4: 3)**

This grace or helping grace is what the Spirit gives us to perform acts of good will for others. These are the 'helps' which God gives us so that we may actually do deeds of love. By actual graces God enlightens our minds to see His ways and strengthens our resolve to walk in them, or to return to them if we have gone astray. His grace does not lessen our freewill and responsibility but increases our freedom. Today I can look back at the events that took place in my life along with the brief encounters that have occurred, and see that it was all a part of my spiritual growth. To be able to, "let the Spirit fly wherever it took me," means that I needed to let it take me where I need to be. Unlike an eagle, there were times when all I could do was walk in pain, failure and fatigue making it impossible to soar or run. Then there were times in my life that I could run and not grow weary but yet could not soar. With patience and persistence I could see results and know I was still in the race. Fr. Bosio, a Salesian priest I met years before Sara's birth, saw that I was at a point in my life where I was running. He just wanted me to keep going without trying to manufacture any spiritual ecstasy, knowing that in time I would soar like the eagles to a place where the currents of God's power would help, carries us on. Fr. Bosio knew that in God's own time, He would show me how He could use me in amazing ways. It took me a long time to realize that only through complete surrender I would be able to climb greater heights. Each and every one of us can soar to that place where we can become productive, and experience the strength and wisdom that comes to us beyond our natural abilities.

Fr. Bosio in his wisdom taught me to live these words and be where I needed to be, **"Let the Spirit fly wherever it takes you"**. The beautiful thing about God is that when I found myself walking, I could rest assured that walking counted with God. I guess that when it's the best you can do—it's enough! God's requirements never exceed the grace He provides. If all I could do is keep one foot in front of the other and follow Him, then I know that He values my walking as much as one's running or soaring.

My closing prayer is that we can all continue to be happy and prosper in future as God intended for us. (Jer. 29:11) *for I know the plans I have for you," declares the Lord, "plans to prosper you and not to harm you, plans to give you hope and a future."*

As you continue to move forward walking, running, or soaring on your path may you always remain connected to God and all those God sends into your life. May you be open to listening and experiencing all the desires of your heart in a personal and profound way. May you find the courage to share your gifts, talents and abilities, creatively and positively. Finally may you discover and share those wonderful and exciting secrets waiting to be heard as you begin to listen with the ears of your heart.

Excerpts taken from Chapter 10, "God's Love in Action," from Cris Smith's Spiritual Writings, "Let the Spirit Fly, Wherever It Takes You."

Journal Writing

Journal writing can be done during your reflection time which can occur either in the morning, evening or whenever you feel prompted to write. There are no rules to your personal journal writing. You simply need to be a "pencil in God's hand", as Mother Teresa would say. Scripture passages and prayers are powerful tools I occasionally use. It gives me a sense of direction at times when I am lost for words. You can get creative and find scriptures or prayers, inspirational sayings, quotes or whatever may move you to write. The key is to simply start writing and to trust the Holy Spirit will fill the pages.

Remember, there are no rules to your journal writing. If you feel you don't know what to write just write down a simple prayer from your heart everyday . . . or maybe something that happened to you . . . or how you are feeling that particular moment. Granted that someone who has never written down his/her prayers, it can become overwhelming, so just begin to write in whatever format you feel comfortable in. The great thing about journal writing is that no matter what you choose to write, at the end, you can finish off by offering it up to the Lord as your prayer.

I have many entries where I neither record Scripture or prayers and go straight to writing my reflections, thoughts, inspirations, questions, concerns, just about anything . . . even my "to do list". Let me also tell you that there are times in my life when I don't get the chance to write for days or weeks, it is then that I ask the Lord to keep those memories impressed on my heart so that when I finally do get a chance to record them the Spirit will help me remember. The key is to simply write when the Spirit moves you.

There are times when the Spirit moves me to write and I begin my journal entry with one line. "Speak Lord, Your Servant is Listening" and then I just write what I hear without stopping to think or edit. These are the entries that I treasure the most

Here are a few reflections to help you get started.

Reflection: What do I really want out of life? Give 3 action words.

For example, Happy, Healthy, Holy

Where do you see yourself in 5, 10, 15 years, or even 20 years from now?

What are my financial goal this year, next year and in 5 years.

What are my family goals?

What are my spiritual goals?

What are my physical goals?

Dream Journal

Don't forget to start a DREAM JOURNAL. You may be someone who has not given much thought to your dreams before or perhaps you have difficulty remembering them the next morning. The great thing about starting a dream journal is that you will begin to remember them if you do just a few things before you go to bed. Simply have a pen and your dream journal close to you so that when you wake up from your sleep you can record any dreams you may recall. The secret is to write then, before you get out of bed and become distracted. Also, before going to bed you can say something like, "Tonight I am going to dream some wonderful and exciting dreams." After recording your dream details in your dream journal you may find that you are feeling more inspired. It can leave you more peaceful if the dream is clear, or it can even leave you with questions if the dream has many symbols attached to them. Take these concerns with you in meditation and see if you can hear a clearer message that is being conveyed to you from within. Remember dreams can be a way of listening to our hearts and listening to God. They can be warning dreams, revelatory dreams, revealing things that you need to address, or events that confirm the direction you are on. They can also be prophetic dreams that give you some insight into the path that you are being called to walk. Perhaps you may even find someone you can share your dreams with and more clarity will surface. If you don't receive any of the above you can simply leave it alone but don't be surprised if weeks, months or even years later you may find yourself in a life experience that may just bring back the memory of a dream you once had long ago. For now simply enjoy your rest and may you have SWEET DREAMS!

For more information about Blue Veil Charity and Sara Elizabeth Centre
Please visit www.blueveil.org
416-747-9796
blueveil@rogers.com

To order CD "Leap of Faith"
Online at www.blueveil.org
Or
Mail a payment of $15.00 plus $10.00 for shipping and handling to
Leap of Faith CD c/o Blue Veil Charity
2110 Kipling Ave. N.
P.O. Box 562, Etobicoke "B"
Etobicoke, On
M9W 5L4

To Order more copies of "The Heart of Listening"
Online at www.blueveil.org
Or
Mail payment of $20.00 plus $10.00 for shipping and handling to
The Heart of Listening c/o Cris Smith
2110 Kipling Ave. N.
P.O. Box 562, Etobicoke "B"
Etobicoke, On
M9W 5L4

PLEASE SHARE:
Is there any personal experience you would like to share that shows how you have come to hear with the ears of your heart? Is there any chapter in this book that you could easily relate to or that sparks a memory that moves you to meditate and reflect? Have you started a journal or do you find that you are drawn to start one? Do you find that you are beginning to recall your dreams? If so, are you recording them and discovering that there is a deeper message behind them? Please feel free to share.
I look forward to hearing from you.
Contact: Cris Smith 416-747-9796 csmith8555@rogers.com

Proceeds go in support of integrated 'arts' based youth programs at the Sara Elizabeth Centre. "Where everyone shines like a star!"

THANK YOU FOR ALL YOUR SUPPORT.

Something About The Author

Cris Smith is a wife, mother, grandmother, teacher, writer, facilitator and one of God's faithful prayer warriors. She worked in the banking industry for over 8 years, working her way up to Loans Officer. She coped with being a working mom for the first four years of her marriage until she and Don her husband, decided to make the necessary changes in their lifestyle so that Cris could become a stay-at-home Mom.

Cris is married to her husband, Don for 34 years now—a mighty long time to collect lots of anecdotes on everyday joys, sorrows, accomplishments, foibles, sacrifices, surprises and even tragedies. Proudly giving birth to nine children, six of which are boys, ranging in ages from 14 to 33, Cris also home schooled three of her children. Unfortunately, shortly after her birth, Sara, their 8th child, passed away.

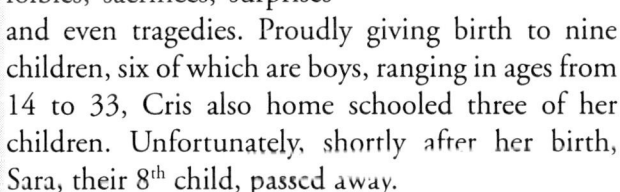

Cris and her family are well known to the Salesian family and have been active members of St. Benedict's Parish since 1982. In 1990, Cris was one of the first members of the Salesian Cooperators in Toronto and held the position of Coordinator for three years. For over 10 years she produced and edited a quarterly magazine called, the Salesian Cooperator Magazine and for the past two years has been writing her spiritual autobiography entitled, **"Let the Spirit Fly Wherever It Takes**

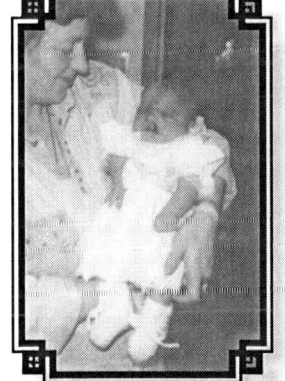

Sara Elizabeth Smith
Born: April 15, 1997
Died: May 11, 1997

You." In the year 2000, Cris was involved with the start-up of a support group called, **SARA'S CORNER,** named in tribute to her baby Sara and facilitated the workshops for parents with babies who had special needs. In 2006 she opened the doors to her own charity that her family founded together under the name **Blue Veil Charity** and became the Executive Director of the charity**.** Today, along with her sons, Cris runs and operates a Centre for youth of all abilities called the **SARA ELIZABETH CENTRE,** named again in tribute to her baby, Sara Elizabeth Smith where young adults with special needs come together to share their gifts and talents through the arts.

Sara's story is filled with many mixed emotions that Cris and her family have been forced to face. The loss of her daughter brought Cris much pain and grief as she searched for answers. Fifteen years ago, Cris did not know what Sara's future held for her but one thing was for sure, she knew that her family was not meant to walk the path alone. Today, she looks back and understands a little better the transformation that had to take place in order for the **Sara Elizabeth Centre** to be born. Cris believes that her family is a big part of God's plan in making themselves one with others, especially those who have been blessed with a special child. Cris Smith exudes joy as she tells her story about Sara.

She understands her role of parenting the Christian way, following the life of Jesus through love, discipline, and above all through complete surrender to His Divine Will.

The message of faith and hope Jesus came to teach her family is experienced through the miracles they have witnessed. In a very personal way Cris allows the reader to become a part of her greatest miracles experienced through God's love in action—His Amazing Grace.

Smith Family picture taken at Matteo (our youngest grandchild's) baptism. The orb that manifested in this picture caught everyone's attention and without a doubt we all felt that it was a sign from Sara who found a way to connect with us. As a mom I feel that this symbol of an orb is just one more way that God uses to speak to our hearts making us aware of His love and grace.

My Family

My Parents and Siblings, taken in 1962.
I am sitting next to my dad.

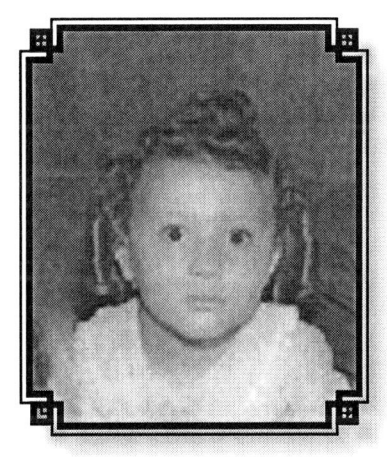

Me at 6 years old. (1962)

Me 50 years later. (2012)

Sara Elizabeth 11 days old.
(April 15th - May 11th 1997)

Dad's 80th birthday.
Starting from left to right, myself, my sister Lucy, Dad, my younger sister Mary, and my brother Frank. Mom passed away fifteen years ago at age 62.

Me and my husband Don
married 33 years (2012)

| Jeff | Phill | Donny | David | Joseph | Jonathan |

My six sons—THE SMITH BROTHERS

My daughters Mary-Ann, Stephanie and me dressed for my son Phill's wedding

My grandchildren Christian, Sabastian and Matteo

My daughter-in-laws Santina and Amber

Journal Reflections

CPSIA information can be obtained
at www.ICGtesting.com
Printed in the USA
LVOW08s0950100317
526721LV00002B/1/P

9 781479 781751